QUEER ASIAN IDENTITIES IN CONTEMPORARY AOTEAROA NEW ZEALAND

One Foot Out of the Closet

Sidney Gig-Jan Wong

QUEER ASIAN IDENTITIES IN CONTEMPORARY AOTEAROA NEW ZEALAND

One Foot Out of the Closet

The Queer and LGBT+ Studies Collection

Collection editor
Seuta'afili Dr Patrick Thomsen

LPp

First published in 2023 by Lived Places Publishing

British Library Cataloguing in Publication Data
A CIP record for this book is available from the British Library

ISBN: 9781915271488 (pbk)
ISBN: 9781915271501 (ePDF)
ISBN: 9781915271495 (ePUB)

The right of Sidney Gig-Jan Wong to be identified as the Author of this work has been asserted by them in accordance with the Copyright, Design and Patents Act 1988.

Cover design by Fiachra McCarthy
Book design by Rachel Trolove of Twin Trail Design
Typeset by Newgen Publishing UK

Lived Places Publishing
Long Island
New York 11789

www.livedplacespublishing.com

Abstract

Sidney Gig-Jan Wong shares his perspectives on his own Queer identities mediated by his Cantonese heritage and upbringing in contemporary Aotearoa New Zealand. The aim of this book is to provide a deep dive into the identity formation process of one individual with the hope that these experiences will enable other Queer people who occupy intersecting marginalisation in society to realise their full potential. This book is intimate, cringy, and challenging, written from the perspectives of a Queer Cantonese man trying to come to terms with his emergent identities.

Key words

Queer; Rainbow; LGBTQIA+; Identity; Community; Migration; Displacement; Racialisation; Reclamation.

Acknowledgements

This book has been in the works for a long time. Many of these stories started off as scribbles in notebooks and odd pieces of writing over the last decade. Who knew they would one day contribute to this book, sharing my most intimate experiences. Firstly, I want to thank my family – Mum, Dad, and my older brother. I also want to say, I'm sorry. I know that things have been complicated over the last few years and I haven't made it any easier being so far from home. If you ever read my book, I want you to know that if I had to do this again, I would've wanted you all there to be by my side. I want to thank my partner, Jake, who has been by my side through thick and thin. You deserve a medal. You have been incredible, thoughtful, and kind. It was such a privilege to meet your parents, and to use that time to craft this book. I can't wait to share our stories one day. I want to thank everyone at Qtopia, Christchurch Heroes, the Ethnic Rainbow Alliance, and the Queer communities of Ōtautahi. I honestly wouldn't be here without their continued support. I want to thank Patrick for giving me this opportunity and guiding me through this process. You're an absolute star. I want to thank all my friends and extended family. I would list you all if I could. I also want to thank my rugby teams, CFC Choppers and the Christchurch Gentlemen, you've taught me to trust myself in a way I never could. Give 'em the chop! Lastly, I want to thank you, the reader. I hope you enjoy reading about my experiences as much as I enjoyed living through them.

Contents

Content warning

This book contains explicit references to, and descriptions of, situations which may cause distress. This includes references to and descriptions of:

- Abuse
- Body hatred and fatphobia
- Death, dying, and mass murder
- Hateful behaviour directed at religious groups
- Homophobia
- Hospitalisation
- Mental illness and ableism
- Nudity
- Racism and racial slurs
- Self-harm and suicidal thoughts, intentions, and actions
- Sexism
- Sexual assault
- Substance use and abuse
- Swear words or curse words
- Transphobia
- Violence

Every effort has been made to provide more specific content warnings before relevant chapters, but please be aware that references to potentially distressing topics occur **frequently** and **throughout** the book.

Learning objectives

1. Demonstrate an understanding of how different social, cultural, political, and environmental contexts mediate individual and societal perceptions of Queer identities.

2. Describe how transcultural and translinguistic expressions of Queerness allow for the re-emergence of Queer identities.

3. Privilege emerging traditional and indigenous understandings of Queer identities while challenging the notion of universality in Queer identity models developed within Western academic frameworks.

4. Think critically about the impacts of (multi-)marginalisation among members of the Queer community who occupy intersecting marginalisation in society.

5. Engage individual lived experiences and perspectives as a vehicle for effective allyship within and outside the Queer community.

Prologue

We were at the Taoist temple. My parents attended the services every Sunday. My brother and I were passing time in the library. We were waiting until the service was over.

"Do you know the story of The Vinegar Tasters?" an older auntie once asked me. She was a volunteer at the temple.

I cocked my head in confusion. I was still incredibly young at the time. The older auntie laughed at me. She gestured me towards her. She pointed to the painting of three old men crouching over a large earthenware pot and she began narrating her story.

***

Long ago, there were three old men wandering through a forest. Suddenly, a large earthenware pot appeared on the road.

The three old men peered into the pot. Inside was a thick, black liquid.

"What's this?" asked the first old man. "It might be sauce. Why would someone leave this in the middle of a forest?"

The first old man who was the most daring. He figured the only way to uncover this mystery sauce was to taste it. He dipped his finger into the mystery liquid and placed it in his mouth.

"Ugh! This sauce is spoilt!" the first old man cried. He puckered his lips, and his face was scrunched up like a pickled plum. "How disgustingly sour!"

Not believing the first old man, the second old man also dipped his finger in the pot to taste the mystery sauce.

"Ugh! You're right!" cried the second old man. "The sauce is disgusting. The sauce is rancid! It's unbelievably bitter!"

After observing the reaction of the first two old men, the third old man pondered for a moment, and then dipped his finger in the pot to taste it.

The first two old men watched him eagerly.

The third old man swished the mystery sauce in his mouth. Left. Right. Left again.

"I see," the third old man whispered under his breath. He stroked his white beard while deep in thought.

"You're both wrong, and you're both right. It's not sour or bitter. This sauce is sweet." "How could this be?" the second old man protested.

"It's because you're both fools! This sauce isn't spoilt or rancid. It's vinegar!" the third old man stated with a childish grin. "You must learn to appreciate it in its natural state."

The third old man chuckled, and all three old men continued wandering through the forest.

***

"Do you understand the moral of the story, Sidney?" the auntie asked me.

I shook my head vigorously. The older auntie smiled and explained.

"The vinegar represents life. The first old man represents our Confucian values. Our life is like a wine, but without discipline it will spoil and turn into vinegar."

"The second old man represents our Buddhist beliefs. Life isn't bitter or sweet. We need to learn how to displace ourselves from this world of suffering."

"The third man represents our Taoist principles. Life is perfect in its natural state. You cannot know what is sweet without equally understand what it is bitter or sour."

"But remember, Sidney. Our values, beliefs, and principles are all important. One cannot exist without the others. Our three teachings are one."

> *The first time I was bit,*
> *I knew my life was never going to be the same.*
> *What I knew was history.*
> *His fangs breached my skin.*
> *Blood was drawn,*
> *and I wanted more.*
> *The fear was knowing I could never turn back.*

Content warning

This chapter contains references to racism and racial slurs; homophobia; transphobia; swear words or curse words; and violence.

The chapter starts overleaf.

Introduction

Ōtepoti, Spring 2022

I was in the Student Union building at the University of Otago in Ōtepoti (Dunedin). I was sitting on a couch with a microphone in my hand.

The drapes behind me were lit with all the colours of the rainbow. I could barely see the faces of the audience in front of me – hundreds of students watched me eagerly.

The host of the night, Kevin, was sitting across from me on the couch. I felt like I was on a first date. Sarwana invited me as a guest speaker. The event was called "All in" and it was hosted by Silverline which is a student-led, student-focused mental health and well-being initiative. I had received a phone call from my high school friend Sarwana a few weeks earlier.

"Sidney!" I heard Sarwana's excitement. "How've you been? It's been ages since we've talked!"

"I'm good! How about you? Still at the university?" I tried to match Sarwana's enthusiasm.

"We're hosting a speaker night colliding race, belonging, and mental well-being," Sarwana told me excitedly. "I want you to speak to our students. Are you keen?"

"Sure, why not?" I replied jokingly. "I don't know if you'll get much value from me as a guest speaker. My stories aren't all that interesting."

"Don't be silly, Sidney!" Sarwana laughed. "It'll be fun! You've changed so much since high school. I think our students will learn a lot from your experience."

"Well, what kind of stories would you like me to share? Do you want to hear about how my parents migrated from Hong Kong? I could talk about my experience of racism in Christchurch." "Do you want me to talk about how I first realised I was Queer? What about my first kiss?"

"Or the people I have met in New Zealand, Hong Kong, and around the world who have helped me understand my Queer identity?"

"I could share my experience of coming out to my parents, my friends, and my work. You probably don't want to hear about the abuse from my ex-partner while I was in Ōamaru." "They're students, right? I could talk to them what it's like being in the closet as a researcher and how understanding my identity has helped me build the courage to chair local and national Queer organisations."

"Thoughts?"

We continued talking on the phone. I did not think much about the event until the organisers sent through the copy of the event website:

"Sidney shares the story of his own coming out as a Queer Cantonese human, as well as the collective coming out of his family and how he navigates what he called 'one foot in and one foot out of the closet.'"

I could also see the list of invited speakers. They were all prominent writers, directors, actors, singer-songwriters, and choreographers.

"Oh, no," I thought to myself. I did not consider myself as particularly creative or talented. "I hope I do not make a fool of myself."

When it was finally time for me to speak, I tried to feel the light of my own sunshine.

"We'd like to know how your experience of being Queer has intersected with your cultural aspects of his life, like what was particularly challenging being a Queer Cantonese human?" Kevin asked me. He was poised with a list of questions.

"Now that's a good question," I paused for a moment to reflect. "Where should we begin?"

Racialised bodies
Te Awakairangi, Autumn 2022

I was born in Te Awakairangi (Lower Hutt) just north of the capital city. Home for me was a sleepy suburb of Taitā along Te Awakairangi (the Hutt River). I have lived in Ōtautahi (Christchurch) for the last decade. I was never meant to be away for this long.

It was a Tuesday afternoon. Dad and I were stuck in bumper-to-bumper traffic. He drove in from Te Awakairangi to pick me up from the office as I was in Te Whanganui-a-Tara (Wellington) for a meeting. Work offered to put me up in a hotel, but I knew my parents would be upset if I didn't go home. Instead, I was staying with them for the night.

Dad is a quiet man, so we drove in silence. I looked out the window at the passing scenery. When we took our exit and crossed the river, we went past rows upon rows of identical state houses. These were nestled in the valley between the river and the bush. Most of them were built by returned soldiers following the Second World War.

The car scrambled up the driveway. We sped past the window paired with lime green shutters which overlooked the street. The off-white exterior walls of the house were stained brown by years of exposure to dust from the quarry across the valley. The car eventually rolled to a creaky stop.

「我返屋企啦.」 (I'm home!) I announced while I got out of the car with my luggage.

I took off my Doc Martens. As usual, I struggled with the laces before I threw them to the ever-growing pile of shoes. When I finally got through the front door, the aroma of rich sauces, fermented beans, and dried herbs assaulted my senses.

「返屋企啦，就食得飯啦。無唔記得裝香.」 (Are you home? Dinner's nearly ready. Don't forget to burn incense.) Mum instructed me from the garage.

「哦.」 (Okay.) I shouted in return.

We offered incense as a way to venerate our Ancestors. We would ask for their protection and guidance through our daily prayers. Our family altar is located in the living room. I lit three sticks of incense as I approached the altar. In the centre of the makeshift altar is a red plaque with the words 「黃門堂上」 (Venerable Wong Ancestors.)

「黃門堂上，保佑黃家上上下下，出入平安，身體健康.」 (I pray to the venerable ancestors who reside above, protect our household, and grant us safe passage and good health.) I chanted and bowed three times before placing the incense sticks in the shrine.

"Who will remember me once I'm gone?" I wondered if my descendants would honour me this way. "What's my legacy?"

I bowed one more time before leaving the altar. The scent of sandalwood clung to my nostrils. As the smoke drifted into the air, my eyes followed the white wisps. I closed my eyes and reflected on the legacy of my forebears and how I came to be here.

My Ancestors come from a region called Lingnan (嶺南) named after the Nanling (南嶺) mountains. This encompasses the present-day provinces of Guangdong (廣東) and Hainan (海南) and the autonomous region of Guangxi (廣西) in Mainland China; Hong Kong (香港); Macau (澳門); and the northern and central provinces of Vietnam. More specifically, I trace my ancestry to the localities of Sze Yap (四邑), Fatshan (佛山), and Tungkun (東莞).

My Ancestors, who lived in this expansive area, established a distinctive way of life known as 嶺南文化 (ling⁵naam⁴man⁴faa³; Lingnan culture). This culture was characterised by the admixture of Indigenous 百越 (baak³jyut⁶; Baiyue) and 華夏 (waa⁴haa⁶; Huaxia) peoples. My *Huaxia* Ancestors originated from the Yellow River Basin. They migrated to the Lingnan region as a result of war and famine. We can still trace the southward journey of my Ancestors by referencing the 族譜 (zuk⁶pou²; genealogical book) of the 黃 (Wong) clan. These meticulously kept volumes of family history include details for over 150 generations of my clan.

Those who lived in this region popularised 飲茶 (jam^2caa^4; Yumcha), 越劇 ($jyut^6kek^6$; Cantonese opera), 南拳 ($naam^4kyun^4$; Southern-style Chinese martial arts), and 舞獅 (mou^5si^1; lion dancing). Beyond these tangible aspects of Lingnan culture, the *Huaxia* also brought with them complex religious belief system combining 儒家 ($jyu4gaa1$; Confucianism), 道教 (dou^6gaau^3; Taoism), and 佛教 (fat^6gaau^3; Buddhism) with folk religious beliefs.

Of the three institutionalised belief systems, Confucianism is definitely the most inflexible. Confucian thought is a complex philosophy with a focus on the five constants of 仁 (jan^4; benevolence), 義 (ji^6; righteousness), 禮 (lai^5; propriety), 智 (zi^3; wisdom), and 信 ($seon^3$; sincerity) and the four virtues of 忠 ($zung^1$; loyalty), 孝 ($haau^3$; filial piety), 節 (zit^3; continence), and 義 (ji^6; righteousness). These rites have maintained discipline and order within families and communities.

On the other end of the philosophical spectrum is Taoism which provides balance to the rigidness of Confucianism. Taoism emphasises the virtues of 無為 (mou^4wai^4; inaction) and 自然 (zi^6jin^4; naturalness). Aspects of life beyond our control could be described as 緣份 ($jyun44fan^6$; predestination) or as I like to call them, fateful coincidences. Taoist practitioners also adhere to the 三寶 ($saam^1bou^2$; three treasures) which include 慈 (ci^5; compassion), 儉 (gim^6; frugality), and 不敢為天下先 ($bat^1gam^2wai^4tin^1haa^6sin^1$; humility).

道 (*dou⁶*; *Tao*) is the fundamental in Taoism. *Tao* can be represented by the太極圖 (*taai³gik⁶tou⁴*; *Yin Yang* symbol). This represents unification of the oppositional, yet complementary forces of 陰 (*jam¹*; *Yin*) and陽 (*joeng⁴*; *Yang*). *Yin* can be described as the passive or negative principles in nature while *Yang* can be described as the active or positive principles in nature. The curvy line represents the non-linear divide between these cosmic energies. The contribution of each force is proportional to the other, one force cannot exist without the other.

Tao is best cultivated within the individual. Fundamentally, we are all the sum of our parts. This is known as 自道 (*zi⁴dou⁶*; the *Tao* of the self) or the personal way of being. The proportion of *Yin* and *Yang* will differ between individuals. Contemporary interpretations have reduced the semiotics of *Yin* and *Yang* to represent feminine and masculine energies. However, this is not entirely true. This is because within *Yin* there is *Yang* and within *Yang* there is *Yin*. *Tao* exists beyond the binary.

The last of these belief systems is Buddhism which is based on the teachings of the Siddhartha Gautama – the Buddha (the awakened). This belief system originated in present-day North India, but it has since been shaped by folk religious beliefs when it arrived in the *Huaxia* heartland. Proponents of Buddhism aim to liberate themselves from earthly attachment by attaining spiritual enlightenment. Those who fail to do so are doomed to 輪迴 (*leon⁴wui⁴*; *samsara*) and face the consequences of 因果 (*jan¹gwo²*; *karma*).

These beliefs allowed my Ancestors to live harmoniously (at times) by cultivating 自道 (*zi⁶dou⁶*; way of the self) and 關係 (*gwaan¹hai⁶*; interpersonal relationships). This syncretic belief system is known as 三教 (*saam¹gaau³*; the three teachings). We are "born Confucian, live Taoist, and die Buddhist". Failure to cultivate these personal and interpersonal relationships will lead to a loss of 面 (*min⁶*; face, esteem) and 臉 (*lim⁵*; face, reputation).

Over generations, Lingnan cultures diversified into recognisable ethnolinguistic groups such as 本地 (*bun²dei⁶*; *Punti*, Cantonese), 客家 (*haak³gaa¹*; Hakka), 蜑家 (*daan⁶gaa¹*; Tanka), and 河老 (*ho⁴lo⁵*; Hokkien), to name a few. We have acquired different identity frameworks to position ourselves within our dynamic culture. We use descriptive terms like 本地人 (bun²dei⁶jan⁴; local) or 外地人 (*ngoi⁶dei⁶jan⁴*; stranger) to establish our identity as native or foreign. However, we also have had to position ourselves as 自己人 (*zi⁶gei²jan⁴*; one of our own) or 外人 (*ngoi⁶jan⁴*; outsider) within our diasporic communities.

Up until the late-twentieth century, the Lingnan region was also known as the "Home of the Overseas Chinese". Some early Ancestors left the homeland for greener pastures across mainland and maritime Southeast Asia. They also had the unfortunate luxury of living on the doorstep of Treaty Ports ceded to the 「八國聯軍」 (Eight-Nation Alliance) following the Opium Wars. As a descendant of my Lingnan Ancestors, their culture and belief systems have had a major influence on my world-view. My heritage is an inalienable aspect of my identity. However, since leaving our homeland, our heritage holds little currency in contemporary Aotearoa. Instead, we are assigned reductive labels such as Chinese or Chinaman, and even a colourful array of slurs. These diminutive categories ignore the complexities of our communities.

In a final act of reduction, our communities have been folded into an aggregated identity, "Asian", through the process of racialisation. US academics first coined this socio-political process "to signify the extension of racial meaning to a previously racially unclassified relationship, social practice, or group" (Omi and Winant, 2015). The definition was further refined with the inclusion of racial formation which is "the sociohistorical process by which racial identities are created, lived out, transformed, and destroyed". Racialisation is grounded in coloniality/imperialism, white supremacy, and anti-Blackness (Karim, 2017).

A similar, yet different, process of racialisation can be observed in Aotearoa. The British colonial administration collapsed societal structures of *tangata whenua* (Indigenous peoples of Aotearoa) such as *hapū* (kinship group), *iwi* (extended kinship group), and *waka* (allied kinship groups) into a singular Māori (native) racial identity (Sankar et al., 2022). In a similar vein, the development of a pan-European Pākehā identity established a white racial identity. This Māori-Pākehā binary racial distinction is a direct product of colonisation. Over time, this Pākehā identity was reconfigured to a raceless settler identity and the dominance of Pākehā whiteness proliferated through the systems and structures of Aotearoa.

While tangata whenua continue to be racialised within this bicultural model of the state, the racial invisibility of Pākehā in society means "for non-white *tauiwi* [non-Māori] this often results in a default assimilation process [which] is facilitated by a human capital model of migration" (Sankar et al., 2022). Asians in Aotearoa, as with other non-white *tauiwi*, are expected to assimilate with the dominant norms of Pākehā whiteness regardless of our diverse social, cultural, or linguistic identities.

This dual heritage enables "the double erasure of Māori *mana motuhake* [self-determination] and of non-white *tauiwi* from the national narrative" (Sankar et al., 2022).

Racialisation enforces white supremacy. It is a continuation of Aotearoa's colonial legacy. Within my community, there is a perception that we are destined to assimilate to whiteness. As our links to the homeland weaken over time, our identities are reduced to our racialised bodies. We inexplicably become outsiders to our own people. Even our language has evolved to distinguish local-born identities such as 土生 (*tou²saang¹*; local born) and 竹升 (*zuk¹sing¹*; bamboo shoot) to indicate our cultural deficiency. But this does not have to be the way. We are only now beginning to understand how race and ethnicity interplay with our complex "emergent identit[ies]" (Pang, 2003). Our identities are a synthesis of the cultures and belief systems of our homeland, our wider diaspora, and our host nation. We have the tools to reclaim our identities.

Queer identities
Ōtautahi, Autumn 2019

I was attending a workshop called *Understanding Sexuality and Gender*. It was facilitated by a prominent Queer organisation that came down from Te Whanganui-a-Tara to educate us, public servants, about sexuality and gender. Like most of the people in the room, I was doing this workshop as part of my professional development, but I was also there out of curiosity. Even though I was part of this Queer community, I still wondered what it meant to be Queer.

The origins of the word Queer are highly contested, but there is evidence of the word being used in place of homosexual, gay, and lesbian since the late-nineteenth century (Jagose, 1996). It did not take long before Queer was popularised as a slur in the twentieth century. The reclamation of Queer as a self-descriptive label for people with diverse expressions of gender, sex, and sexuality is only a recent phenomenon since the 1990s. There are still some people who refuse to associate themselves with this word due to its history with homophobic abuse.

An understanding about the etymology of a word does not guarantee an understanding of a word – to be Queer. In Aotearoa-born Queer academic Annamarie Jagose's monograph, Queer Theory: An Introduction (1996), she explained in academic poetry that "[Q]ueer describes those gestures or analytical models which dramatize incoherencies in the allegedly stable relationships between chromosomal sex, gender, and sexual desire". This definition suggests Queer exists in opposition to norms generated by endosex, cisgender, and heterosexual identities.

Jagose (1996) further contextualised Queer identities within American philosopher Judith Butler's post-structuralist feminist framework whereby "gender operates as a regulatory construct that privileges heterosexuality" in relation to French philosopher Michael Foucault's operations of power and resistance. Although this interpretation of Butler's argument was only in reference to lesbian and gay subject positions, it is implied the deconstruction of gender norms through a Queer lens legitimises non-endosex, non-cisgender, and non-heterosexual identities.

With the expansion of a Queer identity to encompass all people with diverse expressions of sexual orientation, gender identity, gender expression, and sex characteristics, so has the definition of Queer when framed within Western philosophical traditions. Therefore, Queer and "Queer theory and politics necessarily celebrate transgression in the form of visible difference from norms. These Norms are then exposed to be norms, not natures or inevitabilities" (Stewart, 2018). At the most fundamental level, a Queer identity is about deconstructing societal norms which have been ingrained in our systems and structures.

We are still on a journey, both as a community and academically, to understand what it means to be Queer. It is perhaps the vagueness of Queer which gives this ever-evolving identity its social and political currency. The lack of definition resists the academic obsession to classify identities into discrete categories. "It is not simply that [Q]ueer has yet to solidify and take on a more consistent profile, but rather that its definitional indeterminacy, its elasticity, is one of its constituent characteristics" (Jagose, 1996). It is up to us who are part of this ever-evolving community to determine who is one of our own or who is not.

Of course, the workshop did not go into this detail of defining what it means to be Queer or what it means to have a Queer identity.

"These are the words we use for our Rainbow community in Aotearoa."

The facilitator flashed several terms on the screen: Lesbian, Gay, Bisexual, Transgender, Questioning, Intersex, Asexual, and Non-binary.

I was surprised to see Queer was not on that list. Perhaps the facilitators wanted to keep this workshop palatable to the general audience.

"We also have terms specific to our Māori and Pacific Rainbow communities."

Even more words flashed on the screen: *Takatapui*, *Whakawahine*, *Whakatane*, *Tangata ira tane*, *Mahu*, *Vaka sa lewa lewa*, *Palopa*, *Fa'afafine*, *Akava'ine*, *Fakaleiti*, and *Fakafifine*.

"What about our Asian communities?" I asked. I was genuinely curious.

"Well, those terms don't exist – as far as we're aware," the facilitator replied.

"Oh," I was surprised. They seemed quite confident with their answer.

The facilitator saw my quizzical expression and paused briefly to reflect on their answer before they extended their response. My expressions can at times be unintentionally loud.

"I'm sorry, but we haven't actually come across any."

All the attendees, largely Pākehā, nodded their heads affably. I was the only visible Queer person there. I was also the only visible Asian person in the group. I sat there feeling invisible, like I did not exist.

The lack of mainstream terminology does not indicate recognisably Queer identities are absent across Asia. Diverse expressions of sexuality were frequently referenced in Hindu texts (Siker, 2006). These sexual relationships flourished in pre-colonial India and were considered to be "very natural, normal and inevitable emotional aspect of human sexual life" (Parekh, 2003). In dynastic China, accounts of prominent historical figures regularly featured same-sex relationships such as the tender romance between Emperor Ai of Han 漢哀帝 and Dong Xian 董賢 which was immortalised by the idiom 「斷袖之癖」 (passion of the cut sleeve).

However, sexuality is only one facet of Queerness. The presence of diverse expressions of sex and gender can still be observed in communities across contemporary Asia such as *nat kadaw* in Myanmar; *phuying*, *phuying prophet song*, or *phet thee sam* in Thailand; *hijra* in India and across South Asia; *khawaja sara* in Pakistan; and *bissu* of the Bugis people in Indonesia. There is also evidence of gender fluidity in Japan through the practice of *wakashu* and in China where male-identified bodies exclusively in 戲曲 (*hei³kuk¹*; Chinese opera) played 旦 (*daan³*; female roles). It was common practice for these actors to continue presenting as female off-stage.

Despite the illustrious history and continued presence of Queer identities across Asia, Queer people living in Asia experience the highest levels of discrimination, criminalisation and punishment, and intolerance (Lee and Ostergard, 2017). In some cases, the erosion of Queer rights was a direct result of European imperialism and colonisation where former colonies inherited laws criminalising non-cisheteronormative behaviour such as India (Upadhyay, 2020) and Hong Kong (Kong, 2012). The continued enforcement of discriminatory legislation was justified through reinterpretation of traditional values and belief systems.

Even though I was brought up speaking Cantonese, I was never taught to articulate different Queer identities. One of the first words

I learnt was 基 (*gei¹*; gay), which is a phonosemantic borrowing from English. I was later introduced to a laundry list of unsavoury terms to describe recognisably Queer behaviour such as *kem¹* (camp), 型 (*naa²jing⁴*; girly), and 娘娘腔 (*noeng⁴noeng⁴hong¹*; sissy). These insults were grounded in misogyny and were used to emasculate men. Any behaviour that was viewed as non-cisheteronormative lay on the spectrum between 變態 (*bin³taai³*; mentally disturbed) and 雞姦 (*gai¹gaan¹*; to bugger).

When I reflect on my own cultural values, there appeared to be an extreme dissonance between the language used to describe Queer behaviour and my belief systems. Neither Buddhism or Taoism held strong views on diverse expressions of gender, sex, or sexuality (Siker, 2006). In the contrary, there is a dedicated Deity, Tu'er Shen 兔兒神, who oversees the sexual and relationship between men. The only caveat I could identity stems from Confucianism which ensures the maintenance of gender roles and the duty of male heirs to maintain the bloodline. This meant Queer behaviour was generally tolerated within family units, but there was an expectation for offspring.

Of course, the Cantonese I acquired as a heritage language speaker was less refined. Now I have adopted neologisms such as 同性戀 (*tung⁴sing³lyun²*; homosexuality), 雙性戀 (*soeng1⁴sing³lyun²*; bisexuality), 跨性別 (*kwaa¹sing³bit⁶*; transgender), 雙性 (*soeng¹sing³*; intersex), and 疑性戀 (*ji⁴sing³lyun²*; questioning). These terms were coined in the 1950s to facilitate translations for European academic models of gender and sexuality. My lack of native vocabulary to describe these Queer identities in Cantonese might suggest greater cultural and sociolinguistic processes at play – most definitely beyond the scope of this book.

Our current understanding of recognisably Queer identities is framed within Western philosophical frameworks. With this in mind, what is the relevance of Queer within an Asian context? They are similar in the sense that they both resist to be defined. We can easily pose a similar question of what it means to be Asian. Some Queer Asian academics who occupy this space use "Queer, again, not as self-definition of individuals, but as a political denominator for linking sexuality with broader political positions from an intersectional lens" (Al-Ali and Sayegh, 2019).

Black feminist legal scholar Kimberlé Crenshaw coined intersectionality to examine the multidimensionality of Black women's experiences in the US (Crenshaw, 1989). In an interview, Crenshaw described intersectionality as "a lens through which you can see where power comes and collides, where it interlocks and intersects" and was not meant to be a "grand theory of everything" (Columbia Law School, 2017). It is an analytical framework to understand how intersecting identities contribute to experiences of discrimination and privilege. Some identities may include race, class, Indigeneity, ethnicity, religion, disability, gender, and sexuality.

Queer, as it currently stands, is shorthand for deconstructing societal norms through a white lens. Some Queer Asians reject Queer as it is viewed as a foreign term from "the language of the closet", while others embrace these borrowed terms as a way of protecting their communities from conservative societies (Semerene, 2019). Even in my Cantonese, I am moving away from pejorative terms like 基 (gei[1]; gay) to homegrown terms such as 同志 (tung[4]zi[3]; comrade) to establish a recognisably Queer identity accounting for a Punti Hong Kong context. This term was co-opted from Mandarin into Cantonese by Hong Kong-based columnist Michael Lam 林邁克 to trivialise the communist regime to the north (Lau et al., 2017). Only time will tell whether I adopt this new identity framework.

Queer identities are fluid, inclusive, undefined, and ever evolving. Queer Asian identities are even more so. Marathi human rights activist Sharif D. Rangnekar poetically defined what it meant to him as a Queer person, as a Queersapien: "Queerness exists outside the box. It is defined by the indefinite, the expanse, the width and length, the roundness of the Earth. It is coloured by colours. It isn't one colour. So, seeing things from a [Q]ueer standpoint or lens or view isn't about one idea or thought either. It is as diverse as it can get. It recognises that there are many ways to live as many ways to die" (Rangnekar, 2022).

Closet spaces
Ōtautahi, Summer 2022

My partner, Jake, and I were looking for a flat to rent. Jake is English and he moved to Aotearoa when he was a teenager. We have lived together in some shape or form for nearly three years – almost as long as we have been together. When Jake's flat disbanded, we decided to move in together. It felt like the next logical step of our relationship.

We applied for a rental property north of the central city of Ōtautahi. We spent two years building a home together. I was heartbroken the day we received the email from our property manager informing us that we had to move out of our rental in

Edgeware. We had no choice as the owners intended to sell the property in the new year.

We applied for a two-storey townhouse in St Albans close to Edgeware Village. We did not want to move far as we liked the neighbourhood. We were close to Jake's work, I was only a twenty-minute bike ride to the university, our rugby club rooms were nearby, and most of our friends were within walking distance. I affectionately called it "the Gaybourhood".

"You've passed the background check with flying colours. I've spoken to the owner about your condition," the property manager told me over the phone a few days after the viewing.

"What do you mean by our condition?" I was surprised by the odd phrasing.

"What I meant is that I suggest you meet with the owner before you sign anything. She seems uncomfortable with your … arrangement," the property manager clarified.

"Bugger." I was in disbelief. This was the first time I had encountered a problem with my same-sex relationship. "Sure, we can meet the owner tomorrow afternoon."

"Where are you from?" the owner asked me when Jake and I arrived at the townhouse. She was a middle-aged Pākehā woman.

"Well, I grew up in Wellington," I replied honestly.

"No, where are you really from?" the owner insisted.

I realised in that moment that she had no interest in my upbringing. What she wanted to know was why I spoke with a New Zealand English accent, but I was not "white".

"Great," I thought to myself. "Not only is the owner homophobic, she's also racist."

At this point, Jake was seething. After three years of being in a relationship together, he knew when I thought something was not right. Microaggressions like when she refused to shake my hand but had no problems greeting Jake. No one asked Jake where he was from.

"You know what, I'd like to look over the paperwork again before signing," I suggested to the owner and the property manager.

Jake understood this to mean "Let's get the fuck out of here", so we gathered our paperwork and promptly vacated the property. There are some battles that are not worth fighting. This just happened to be one of the many countless examples of racism and homophobia I have experienced as a Queer Asian person in contemporary Aotearoa.

In this book, I share my perspectives on my on Queer identity, and how this identity has been mediated by my Cantonese heritage and upbringing in Aotearoa. It was these seemingly inconsequential interactions which have made the greatest impact on how I navigate this lived place. I have deliberately used the terms Asian and Queer to describe my identity. I could have chosen more nuanced terminology to describe my identity, but I chose not to because being Queer and Asian are intrinsically linked to my experience in Aotearoa.

The closet I refer to in the title of this book refers to the systemic and structural barriers that discourage an individual from disclosing their Queer identities. These closet spaces can exist as a physical or metaphysical construction. For example, discrimination, unconscious bias, and legislation criminalising Queer behaviour are all forms of systems and structures used to enforce cisheteronormative behaviour.

Brown (2005) examined closet spaces within built landscapes and found that the closet is "a term used to describe the denial, concealment, erasure, or ignorance of lesbians and gay men [et cetera]. It describes their absence – and alludes to their ironic presence nonetheless – in a society that, in countless interlocking ways, subtly and blatantly dictates that [cisgenderism and] heterosexuality is the only way to be."

The closet can also be perceived as state of being where individuals may either remain closeted or to come out of the closet. Some benefits of coming out include improved psychological well-being, increased self-esteem, decreased distress, diminished risky behaviour, improved interpersonal relations, and enhanced relatedness to key institutions such as in the workplace (Corrigan and Matthews, 2003).

On the other hand, the cost of coming out includes physical harm, social avoidance by others, social disapproval, and increased self-consciousness. However, this framing of the closet and Queer identity formation is grounded in Eurocentric individualism as it suggests that there is personal choice in remaining closeted or coming out.

There is a growing need to re-examine the universality of the coming out process as it is innately a "Westernised, white, cisgender, gay, male" experience (Han, 2009). This is because people who occupy intersecting marginalisation in society may also occupy multiple closets and may continue to experience systemic and structural barriers.

Thomsen (2021) interviewed Korean American gay men living in Seattle through *talanoa* (dialogue) to examine their coming out process. Some of these gay men developed an adaptive tool described as a narrative of convenience to defer the need to come out so they could continue to weave between their sexual identity and their families.

These gay men developed this adaptive tool based on necessity as a result of their cultural values, migration pressures, and their communities mediated through the lens of Christianity. However, some of these gay men rejected the narrative of convenience by coming out publicly as they no longer wanted to be associated with the wider Korean American community.

Some Aotearoa-based academics are considering related processes such as letting in as a more realistic framing of the coming out process for individuals within our Queer and Ethnic communities Nakhid et al. (2022). The concept of letting in originated from diasporic Queer People of Colour in the US. By bringing families into the closet, Queer individuals can co-construct their identity with their family and community.

This letting in process enables the maintenance of interpersonal relationships and conflict avoidance, and acknowledges the importance of status in the community of their family. Whether someone chooses to come out or let in, the path to living an authentic life may not be a straightforward process. Progress is not linear or chronological and people may have found themselves one step out of the closet like I have throughout my experience.

In this book, I have adopted an autoethnographic approach to understand how I have navigated the coming out process as a person who occupies intersecting marginalisation. This approach was championed by Adams (2011) who examined his own lived experience of the closet. Like Adams (2011), I have included personal experience; anonymised informal and unsolicited conversations; and mass-mediated representations of Queer Asian identities.

My intention for this book is not to contribute to sociological theory or to create a guide on how Queer Asians come out/let in in contemporary Aotearoa. Furthermore, this book is not meant to uncover some universal thread that weaves the estimated 19,500 Queer Asian adults in Aotearoa together (Stats NZ, 2022). Instead, the purpose of this book is to provide a deep dive into the ongoing identity formation process for just one of these individuals – mine.

Content warning

This chapter contains references to body hatred and fatphobia; death, dying, and mass murder; mental illness and ableism; sexism; racism and racial slurs; and violence.

The chapter starts overleaf.

1
to leave one's homeland

Ōtautahi, Summer 2020

Most Mondays, I would go to Te Toka on Peterborough Street to pack condoms. This was the office and testing centre for the New Zealand AIDS Foundation (NZAF) in Ōtautahi. Recently, NZAF changed their name to the Burnett Foundation Aotearoa, and they are now based in Phillipstown. I have only been back once since the move.

Condom packing was never the most exciting of volunteering activities, but I enjoyed the company of the other volunteers and the NZAF always provided snacks. Condoms are still one of the best tools to keep our communities safe from HIV and other sexually transmitted diseases.

I grabbed a cardboard sleeve, one condom, one packet of lubricant that was too big, and pressed them together. Perhaps this was karma for all the condoms I had unpacked over the years.

"Could you please help me organise an event for our Asian communities during Christchurch Pride? We want to increase our engagement with Asians. I'm really struggling to think of something," Darren asked me one Monday afternoon.

Darren was working at the NZAF at the time. I met him while playing touch rugby with the Christchurch Heroes.

"Do you have any ideas?" I asked Darren to clarify.

"How about something cute? We could use the space at Te Toka," Darren suggested.

"What event would cater to most of our Asian communities?" I brainstormed quietly as I continued to pack the envelopes. I inspected one of the parcels and then had an idea. "We could wrap dumplings?"

Dumplings exist in different forms across Asia. There are *gyoza* from Japan, *jiaozi* from Mainland China, and *momo* from Nepal and India.

"Sounds great," Darren replied. "How about a test run next week?"

Darren and I met the next week to go to "Chinatown" – a cluster of shops in Church Corner with a high concentration of Chinese supermarkets, restaurants, and takeaways – to buy some ingredients to make some dumplings.

"Don't you think we've got a great gay scene?" Darren exclaimed as we headed to his car.

"Well, it can be tough if you're Asian," I admitted to Darren.

"What do you mean?" Darren sounded confused.

"You've never come across the phrase 'no fats, femmes, or Asians' on Grindr?" I asked. I was surprised he had never heard of this.

"Never," Darren replied rather bluntly. "I guess it's not a problem that affects me."

Darren picked up two other volunteers on the way to my inner-city apartment. They were also happy to show Darren how to make dumplings. Dennis was Chinese from the Central Plains. His friend, Harry, was also Chinese from the Northeast. My family was from the South.

My dumplings were packed to the brim with pork, shrimp, and chives. Dennis was familiar with a filling comprised of port, rice noodles, and scrambled eggs. Harry held a firm stance that the only appropriate filling for dumplings was beef. Each style reflected the diet of our Ancestors.

Darren thought that this was going to be a straightforward exercise. He could not have found three people any more different than us three. How were we meant to organise one event to unify our "Asian" communities?

As the three of us sat there making our own style of dumpling, we started sharing our back stories. We talked about how we came to be in Ōtautahi.

"I'm originally from China," Dennis told me. "I came here as an international student."

"Same here," Harry nodded in agreement.

"I was born in New Zealand," I told the other two. "Mum came here as a skilled migrant." We took a moment to reflect on the multitude of fateful coincidences that had had to occur for us to be in that room together.

"I'm married," Dennis told me. He showed me his wedding band. It was a simple gold ring. "I've met his family. They're really nice people."

"Has your husband met your family?" I asked Dennis curiously.

"No," Dennis replied. He let out a sigh and continued wrapping his dumplings. "My family doesn't know I'm married to a man. At least my family are in China. I can be myself here."

Despite our differences, Dennis, Harry, and I felt like we shared a common understanding. There is a Confucian saying, 「溫故而知新」 (to recall the past to understand the future). Perhaps if we wanted to know what it meant for us to be Queer, and as we had very distinct expressions of being a Chinese person in Aotearoa, we should look to our past in order to understand our future.

Yellow peril
Haehaenui, Winter 2013

As much as my heritage is an important aspect of me, I only started learning about the history of Chinese communities in Aotearoa in the second year of university. I was taking a course called "Kiwi Culture". The purpose of the course was to explore the invention of Kiwi culture. Some key questions addressed in the course included: "How has national identity formed?", "Who is a 'New Zealander' and who is excluded from dominant concepts of nation?", "What aspects of culture are Indigenous and how much of it is copied from overseas?"

"I'd like you to research an aspect of Kiwi culture," my lecturer instructed us.

I looked through the topic list: "Assess Sir Edmund Hillary's appeal as a Kiwi icon", "Critically evaluate the evolution of New Zealand's culinary traditions", "What is unique about Kiwiana?", "An essay on a topic of your own choosing".

"Can I research about the history of Chinese communities?" I asked my lecturer.

"Of course, you can!" my lecturer replied enthusiastically. "Can you think of how Chinese Kiwi culture differs from mainstream Kiwi culture?"

I spent my whole life never realising Cantonese, Chinese, and Asian identities were valid interpretations of Kiwi identity. How could I be so naive? It made complete sense to me that my identity is an aspect of Kiwi culture. This prompted me to research the history of our Chinese communities so I could better understand my own identity.

My curiosity to uncover this forgotten history brought me to the banks of the Haihainui (Arrow River) in the small settlement of Haehaenui (Arrowtown). This town was once the economic heart of the Otago gold rush. In the Lakes District, summers are cool and dry while winters are cold and harsh. As we venture away from the historic gold mining town, we come across a collection of ruins and small huts carved into the hill. This is the historic Chinese settlement, and one of the few reminders of our forgotten histories and the first significant period of migration of Chinese to Aotearoa which began in nineteenth century (Butler, 1977).

Many Cantonese had no choice but to leave the Lingnan homeland as a result of social and political unrest (Ng, 1962). At the time, many European miners left the region, as finds in the goldfields became increasingly rare. The provincial government believed they could solve this labour shortage issue by exploiting cheap experienced Chinese miners who were desperate to support their families. They were welcomed with open arms and officials assured "that the Mongols shall be protected on their arrival" (The Otago Witness, 30 September 1865).

These Cantonese men saw themselves as sojourners – temporary visitors, yearning for home. This factor was important, as the politicians did not want to threaten the colony's white New Zealand reputation. However, the enthusiasm of the provincial government waned within a decade. Resentment towards the Cantonese miners in Aotearoa grew and the central government passed legislation to restrict the movement of Chinese communities. This was known as the Yellow Peril (Ip and Murphy, 2005). The Chinese Immigrants Act 1881 restricted the number to one Chinese per ten tonnes of cargo with an added levy of £10 per person and was further increased to one Chinese per two hundred tonnes of cargo with an added levy of £100 when the Chinese Immigrants Amendment Act 1888 came into force (Lai, 1974). In today's currency, this is equivalent to NZ$2,000 and NZ$25,000, respectively.

At the turn of the century, gold became scarce and many of these men were too old to make the journey back to China. Many left in search of gold elsewhere, while some remained and moved north to the main centres. The discriminatory immigration laws made it uneconomical for Chinese communities to send extended family members to Aotearoa. By 1896, women made up only two per cent of the Chinese populations (Butler, 1977). These laws effectively created a bachelor society. They were effectively trapped in Aotearoa with no means of returning home.

It was the middle of winter when I visited the historic Chinese settlement. The ground was frozen and a thick layer of frost had formed on the huts. Hoar frost hung from the tree branches like chandeliers glistening under the midwinter sun. As I wandered through the ruins and the reconstructed huts, I tried to imagine what it was like for these men to be alone and so far from home. I imagined them huddling together for warmth as they dreamt of one day returning to the warm climate of Lingnan.

The invasion and occupation of East Asia by the Imperial Japanese Army during the Second World War accelerated the establishment of Chinese communities in Aotearoa. 249 women and 244 children of former miners were given permission to migrate to Aotearoa to avoid this conflict in 1939 (Ng, 1962). They were allowed in the country on a temporary basis, but the successive government allowed these families to remain in Aotearoa. For the first time in nearly a century, the change in mentality from sojourner to settler meant a local-born Cantonese community began to emerge (Ip, 1990).

I know of extended family who migrated to Te Awakairangi in the 1940s under these circumstances. The descendants of these Chinese families were still perceived as a threat to Aotearoa's white New Zealand reputation as they would now receive the same rights as British New Zealanders (Murphy, 2003). Even though these families were legally entitled to be here, they were still not welcome.

Eternal migrants

Unlike 老華僑 (lou⁵waa⁴kiu⁴; old Chinese migrants) who arrived during the gold rush era, my parents were part of the second wave of Cantonese migrants to come to Aotearoa. They left Hong Kong in the late 1980s to settle in Te Awakairangi where we already had family. We are a classic example of chain migration. Like the first wave of Cantonese migrants, my recent family history has been intricately linked with colonisation, displacement, and migration.

本地 (*bun²dei⁶*; Punti (客家(*haak³gaa¹*; Hakka), 蜑家 (*daan⁶gaa¹*; Tanka), and 河老(*ho⁴lo⁵*; Hokkien) have lived side by side in what would be the colony of Hong Kong "since time unknown". This colonial project occurred in three acts. The Qing Empire first ceded sovereignty of Hong Kong Island to the British Empire following its defeat in the First Opium War in 1841 and 1842. The British colony was extended to the Kowloon Peninsula following the Second Opium War in 1860. Finally, the British Crown obtained a 99-year lease from the Qing Empire for the New Territories in 1898. My great-grandparents and grandparents fled to the colony of Hong Kong through the Portuguese colony of Macau to escape famine and political turmoil following the fall of the Qing Dynasty in 1912 and the looming Chinese Civil War.

Dad's family settled in Kowloon while Mum's family settled on Hong Kong Island. Not long after they were displaced from their 鄉下 (*hoeng¹haa⁶*; ancestral village), the Imperial Japanese Army attacked Hong Kong in 1941 and my family lived under Japanese occupation for nearly four years. When my grandfather was still alive, he recalled the atrocities conducted by the Imperial Japanese Army. An estimated 10,000 people in Hong Kong were executed while many more were tortured, raped, or mutilated under Japanese administration. Food was scarce and the only food source available was sweet potatoes. My Grandpa still refused to eat sweet potatoes until the day he died. The

Japanese occupation of Hong Kong ended in 1945 when Japan surrendered to Allied Forces and the territory was once again a colony of the British Empire.

Peace was short-lived when the Chinese Civil War resumed across the region. This conflict was between the Kuomintang-led government of the Republic of China and the forces of the Chinese Communist Party supported by the Soviet Union. The Chinese Communist Party established the People's Republic of China (PRC) following their victory in 1949. Many Cantonese communities settled in Hong Kong and Macau were now separated from their ancestral villages across the border. As the communist regime progressed, the Cultural Revolution launched by Mao Zedong 毛澤東 in 1966 saw the destruction of cultural and heritage sites across the Cantonese homeland. This revolution also saw a massive change in the spiritual, political, and linguistic systems of traditional Lingnan society on Mainland China with the promotion of state-atheism and Putonghua. Cantonese culture and language continued to thrive in Hong Kong under the colonial administration of the British Empire. Both my parents were born in this period of economic and cultural prosperity.

The question of Hong Kong's sovereignty was raised in the late 1970s when the 99-year lease for the New Territories was coming to term. Diplomatic negotiations were held between the UK and the PRC without the input of those living in Hong Kong at the time. These negotiations resulted in the 「中英聯合聲明」 (Sino-British Joint Declaration) which was signed in 1984. The treaty agreed to transfer the sovereignty of Hong Kong to the PRC. It guaranteed that the economic and political systems of Hong Kong would remain unchanged for 50 years. This was known by 「一國兩制」 (one country, two systems).

The student-led pro-democracy protests throughout Mainland China in 1989 provided a beacon of hope for many Hongkongers. They believed that life would indeed remain unchanged following the handover of sovereignty in 1997. The subsequent Tiananmen Square massacre was a stark reminder as to why many Cantonese fled their ancestral homes for Hong Kong in the first place. This is now known as 「六四事件」 (the June Fourth Incident). The fate of Hongkongers was sealed decades earlier when both Hong Kong and Macau were removed from the United Nations' list of non-self-governing territories in 1972 at the request of the PRC. It is unlikely that Hong Kong will ever experience full sovereignty.

Everyday Hongkongers, like my parents, had the choice to either stay and experience their rights and freedoms being eroded over time or leave. It was under these uncertain conditions that Mum took the opportunity to leave Hong Kong and migrate to Aotearoa as a skilled migrant. We grew up in a working-class household. When my parents left Hong Kong, they left their family, friends, and culture. The only remnants of our heritage were our Cantonese language and belief system.

「你係廣東人你一定要識講廣東話 (You are Cantonese, you must know how to speak Cantonese.) Mum would often remind my brother and me. My parents were adamant that they wanted us to know our language and heritage.

In my Plunket book, which is a guidebook given to parents produced by Aotearoa's largest support service for children under five and their families, they explicitly warned my parents that if they wanted their children to be successful in this new country, they must only speak to their children in English. The prevailing advice at the time was that children of non-English-speaking migrants must speak English and only English at home. This was reiterated by my primary school teachers who believed that acquiring Cantonese would be a disadvantage to my English-speaking abilities. Neither our healthcare providers nor educators believed there was any value in speaking a non-English minority language in Aotearoa.

My parents, with their strong sense of Cantonese heritage, ignored this official advice. They instilled strict language policies at home like an English jar to make sure we only spoke Cantonese at home. This was not the case for many Cantonese from my generation who could no longer speak our shared heritage language because of this unofficial "Speak English" policy. My parents' tenacity enabled my brother and me to continue to speak the language of our Ancestors.

Model minorities

Mum was fortunate enough to immigrate to Aotearoa as a skilled migrant working in manufacturing. This was following the immigration reforms of 1987 due to the exodus of skilled workers from Aotearoa for Australia (Henderson, 2003). She was an experienced tailor in Hong Kong and these skills were well sought after by the local manufacturing industry. After gaining residency, she met Dad in Hong Kong and they have been settled in Te Awakairangi ever since.

The 1990s were a tough period for the Cantonese communities in Aotearoa. Even though the discriminatory policies targeting Asians and specifically Chinese peoples were now removed, racism persisted in the form of discrimination and microaggressions. Anti-Asian and anti-Chinese sentiment in Aotearoa worsened through political discourse mediated by the media. The former leader of the New Zealand First Party, Winston Peters, first coined the "Asian invasion" and continued to preach "New Zealand for New Zealanders". In this case, racialised Asians were not considered real New Zealanders despite citizenship or visa status. Once again, the visible otherness from people from Asian countries were perceived as a threat. Coming to Aotearoa was both a blessing and a curse for my family. On the one hand, my parents were able to escape the political uncertainties of Hong Kong following the handover, but on the other hand, they arrived penniless and relied on the few connections they had in Te Awakairangi.

In order to avoid unwanted attention, my parents' generation were taught not to be tall poppies and to fly under the radar. The tall poppy syndrome is where Pākehā society supports collective mediocrity and opposes individual exceptionalism. It wouldn't be wise to tarnish our reputation as a model minority. When Mum started her first manufacturing job in Te Awakairangi, her line manager would constantly remind her to slow down and to be conscious of her colleagues around her who might feel bad about their productivity.

「你要勤力，但係唔好太勤力.」(You need to be hardworking, but don't be too hard working.) Mum told us as children.

My early childhood was full of happy memories. Our house was always full of food and laughter. Mum was a skilled tailor and made a lot of clothes for me and my brother. On rare occasions, we would go to the tourist hot spots of Taupo and Rotorua when we had family or friends visiting from Hong Kong. Occasionally, we would drive out to Rangiwhakaoma (Castle Point) in the Wairarapa. Nevertheless, Mum's manufacturing career did not last long after she gave birth to me. Our fortunes took a turn for the worse when Mum got sick. This was a pivotal moment in my childhood. At the time, Dad worked as a kitchen hand at the Chinese takeaway owned by our extended family. This was hardly enough for us to support the growing needs of our small family. We also relied heavily on government benefits and money we borrowed from family and friends.

Both my parents struggled to find a sense of community in Te Awakairangi. Mum found it especially difficult to find a sense of belonging outside the Cantonese community. She was used to having all her family and friends around her back in Hong Kong. Dad was a quiet man, while Mum was extremely outgoing. For a while, we were heavily involved with the Taoist temple in Te Awakairangi. The Taoist temple was located in a repurposed four-bedroom house. Even though it was not extravagant, it gave my parents a sense of community.

It did not take long before the demands outweighed the benefits of being part of the temple community. Mum's mental health began to deteriorate because of social isolation and pre-existing health issues. Our local-born Cantonese-speaking family doctor diagnosed Mum with depression and anxiety. I did not understand what that meant, but I just knew that Mum was unwell. My brother and I were now responsible for looking after the house while Dad worked.

For a period in high school, we hand-washed our clothes because we could not afford a new washing machine when ours broke. We survived a decade on Dad's meagre pay before he was offered a job at our local supermarket. Both my brother and I were put to work as soon as we could, especially if we wanted to afford luxuries like school uniforms and class trips. Outside of Mandarin language classes every Sunday, extracurricular activities were out of the question. At first, my brother and I helped out at our extended family-owned Asian supermarket. We would go there every day after school. I was later offered a paid job at a family friend's Asian takeaway. I was not particularly good at either job – I was told I lacked the work ethic – but I was grateful I could contribute to the household. My first legitimate job was at McDonald's. I started on the counter. I was eventually offered a role as a barista in the cafe.

This is what I remember most about my later childhood. I often reflect on my humble beginnings to where I am now as a PhD student surrounded by luxuries. My family lived pay cheque to pay cheque. In hindsight, this worked to my advantage as I always had t excuse. I did not have time to explore relationships and my parents were quite happy with that as well as wanting us to focus on ourselves and our family before divesting our time on other people. We were either working or studying. Perhaps it was a blessing that I did not have time to think about my Queer identity.

Content warning

This chapter contains references to body hatred and fatphobia; death, dying, and mass murder; homophobia; mental illness and ableism; nudity; racism and racial slurs; sexual assault; substance use and abuse; swear words or curse words; transphobia; and violence.

The chapter starts overleaf.

2

to lay roots in the soil

Mumbai, Winter 2023

Sophia and I were the only ones left from our group who had spent our weekend at a music festival. The two of us were sitting on a park bench overlooking the Arabian Sea. Sophia is a Bengali journalist based in New Delhi. Like me, she was also a tourist in Mumbai. We were both trying to figure out what we could do with our last day in this city.

The sun was struggling to break through the thick fog. I am used to the fog back home in Ōtautahi. During the depths of winter, the air would settle at night and cover the plains like a duvet. I like to imagine that this is how it would feel for me to walk through a cloud. The fog never lasts long. By the time the sun rose above the horizon, it would disappear like it was never there. Not here. In Mumbai, the fog lingers and mixes with the smoke in the air.

"There's not much to do in Mumbai, is there?" Sophia remarked as she took out a packet of cigarettes. "There's definitely more to see in New Delhi."

We watched people put out their laundry on the exposed rocks along the coast. The imposing Sea Link hovered in the distance. At this point in the afternoon, it was too late for us to go anywhere. The traffic in Mumbai is notoriously bad. It would have taken us at least an hour to get to downtown Mumbai.

"I'm pretty sure we can't smoke here," I said as I quickly glanced over my shoulder. We were at Jogger's Park in Bandra West. I had a good sense of the socioeconomic index of an area by the number of recreational joggers. By my count, this was a very affluent suburb of Mumbai. Even as a tourist, I felt too poor to be there.

"Who cares!" Sophia laughed as she lit a cigarette in front of me. "What's the worst they can do?" I watched her coolly take a drag from her cigarette. She flicked her hair to the side, revealing the shaved portion of her head. With her white blouse and matching black pants, she definitely looked the part of a journalist.

"Would you like a puff?" Sophia asked me as she passed me her cigarette.

"Sure, why not?" I said as I took a drag of her cigarette. As I took a deep breath, I felt the cool menthol rushing in to fill the cavities of my lungs. I knew I shouldn't be smoking, but after a week in India, I realised a cigarette was inconsequential to the amount of pollution I had already been exposed to.

I was not meant to go to the music festival. This happened by chance. I was in Mumbai for Akhil's wedding. His family is Kutchi, and he grew up in Mumbai. We met while he was in

Ōtautahi and I promised Akhil that I would be there to celebrate his special day.

"Well, what are you going to do after the wedding?" Neil asked me during the *hast melap*. "You're more than welcome to go to Kochi alone and cry about your ex-boyfriend, or you can come with me and my friends to Lollapalooza and not be miserable!"

Like Sophia, Neil's also Bengali. He is very solutions-driven, and he does not have time for indecisive people. He has the perfect temperament for someone who manages a cricket team in New Delhi. Neil's abrasive honesty is what I like most about him.

Besides Neil, my connection with Sophia is that we are both Queer. I was quite open with my Queerness with Neil's friends, and they did not seem to mind. I can't be sure when she came out to me, but I think it must've been when we were all crammed into a taxi trying to get back to Bandra West after the first night of the music festival.

It felt like an act of fateful coincidence that Sophia and I were sitting on that park bench sharing a cigarette that Monday afternoon. Queer people always have a way of finding each other in the most extraordinary circumstances.

"People think I'm strange for being open about being bisexual and polyamorous." Sophia confessed. "I'm lucky I'm in the position I am now, if I came from a different caste, I wouldn't be so fortunate."

"My husband took a long time to process my Queerness." Sophia continued.

"Your husband?" I choked mid-inhale of the cigarette.

"It's not a big deal," Sophia laughed at my reaction. "Lots of people are married. It made him happy and now I can live my life. He's hopelessly in love with me. Do you want to see some photos of the wedding? I was wearing twenty fucking kilos of jewellery that day."

Sophia showed me her wedding photos on her phone.

"I don't think we'd be that open-minded in New Zealand. I feel like our Asian communities are stuck in the past," I told Sophia. "I think we forgot the world changes."

"Do you want to hear a joke?" I asked Sophia.

"Sure," Sophia nodded.

"One fish told the other fish, 'the water's cold today'. The other fish looked surprised and stopped swimming in its tracks. 'What's water?' the other fish replied in terror."

Sophia spluttered and choked on her Limca.

"That's a good one. I'll need to use it in my writing sometime."

"I guess sometimes when we're immersed in a particular way of being, we don't realise until we observe it from a distance," I reflected pensively. I watched the waves crash on to the shore.

"So, tell me about New Zealand," Sophia asked me curiously. She took another drag from her cigarette before she passed the rest of her packet to me. "What is it like being Queer and Asian in New Zealand?"

Unnatural acts
Te Whanganui-a-Tara, Autumn 2021

I was in Te Whanganui-a-Tara in the executive wing, also known as 'the Beehive' of the New Zealand Parliament Building. The parliament complex played host to the second national Cross Agency Rainbow Network (CARN) conference. CARN is a coalition of Queer employee-led networks across the public service. I was there as a member of my agency's Diversity and Inclusion Working Group.

I was surprised I was still invited after I kicked up a fuss about the inequity of the conference. I raised the issue that the event disadvantaged public servants who were not based in Te Whanganui-a-Tara. The inhibitory cost of the conference registration meant those who arguably needed this networking opportunity the most would not be able to access it.

On the second day of the conference, all attendees of the conference were invited to see the 'Rainbow Room' as a special treat. This was one of the six themed select committee meeting rooms which was dedicated to the Queer communities of Aotearoa. We were asked to arrive early to watch a special screening of *Rainbow Voices of Aotearoa New Zealand: A Documentary Short Film* (2019) before we were escorted to the "Rainbow Room".

I waited patiently in line as one of the many attendees. When it was finally my turn to enter the room, I was struck by the tukutuku panel which took centre stage of the room. It was woven with colours from the rainbow and aptly named *Mana takatapui* (2012). It was created by activist, artist, academic, and now Member of Parliament (MP), Dr Elizabeth Kerekere. On the left of the artwork was the Flag of New Zealand and to the right was the *Tino Rangatiratanga* flag. Further to this, Pride flags representing different communities lined the select committee room.

I stood there admiring the tukutuku panel, and for a brief moment, I felt proud – an arrogant sense of pride that few government institutions in the world acknowledged the existence of our Queer communities. Meanwhile, I was brought back to earth when I remembered that I lied to my parents as to why I was in Te Whanganui-a-Tara.

Six framed documents hung from the walls hidden behind a stack of chairs: the Homosexual Law Reform Act 1986 introduced by Labour MP Dame Fran Wilde, the Human Rights Act 1993, the Civil Union Act 2004 introduced by Labour MP David Benson-Pope, the Relationship (Statutory References) Act 2005, the Marriage (Definition of Marriage) Amendment Act 2013 introduced by Labour MP Louisa Wall, and the Criminal Records (Expungement of Convictions for Historical Homosexual Offences) Act 2018.

In a similar way to how Chinese communities were heavily controlled by the state, Queer communities were still heavily regulated by the government of Aotearoa through discriminatory legislation until the late-twentieth century. These documents represented the constitutional milestones towards Queer liberation in Aotearoa. This was evidence of Aotearoa's continued struggle with Queer liberation. The most recent addition is the Conversion Practices Prohibition Legislation Act 2022 introduced by Labour MP Kris Faafoi.

I chuckled to myself when I realised that these documents, which represented significant milestones towards Queer liberation, were hidden behind surplus furniture. Māori have long accepted fluidity in gender and sexuality (Kerekere, 2017). These individuals were sometimes known as *takatapui* which is inclusive of Māori with diverse genders, sexualities, and sex characteristics. The arrival of European missionaries and puritans in the 1800s saw the suppression of takatapui identity. Buggery (or sodomy) became illegal, thereby criminalising homosexuality when Aotearoa inherited the British legal system.

This intolerance by Pākehā society towards diverse sexualities was extended to the Chinese settlers at the time. In one newspaper, the 'yellow peril' was stylised as an octopus-like creature sporting a queue with monstrous features wrapping its tentacles around New Zealand personified by a *wahine Māori* (Māori woman) in distress (New Zealand Truth, 16 February 1907 as cited in Ip and Murphy (2005)). Each tentacle represented the purported evils that these "aliens" brought with them to the colony: greed, licentiousness, brutality, opium, evil habits, and traffic. Unsurprisingly, licentiousness referred to the "heathen practice" of sex between men (Ng, 2003).

A number of homophobic laws were legislated by the colonial government in response to the Yellow Peril, such as the introduction of the Criminal Code Act of 1893 which included the resort to cat-o'-nine-tails for "unnatural acts" (Ferguson, 2003). Similar laws were enacted in other settler-colonies such as Australia and the United States of America to curb the migration of Chinese settlers (Chung and Wegars, 2005). Convictions of Chinese settlers for buggery and bestiality more than doubled in the preceding two decades (Eldred-Grigg, 1984).

In the same way Queer communities have learnt to navigate the closet in Pākehā dominated society, Asians and other racialised communities have also embarked on a similar journey – albeit with much less success. It is by no incident that ethnic enclaves like Chinatowns do not exist in Aotearoa (Yee, 2003). Invisibility is a survival mechanism developed to ensure maximal safety. As I spent more time learning about the history of our Queer and Asian communities, I realised that the closet was a shared experience between our two communities.

The stories of my Queer and Asian forebears were erased from our national histories as they were viewed by Pākehā society as immoral. Members of our Queer communities in Aotearoa are still susceptible to experiencing discrimination and intolerance, especially those who occupy intersecting marginalisation (Lee and Ostergard, 2017). When Queer Asians like me are outspoken about our experience of racism and homophobia, we are a stark reminder of our historical oppression for our "unnatural acts".

Role models
Cologne, Summer 2012

I was in Germany for the International Geography Olympiad. It was my first trip abroad without my family. I was walking with a group of students on the streets of Cologne when I saw shirts on display in a store window. One shirt said, GAY OKAY. The other shirt said, BOYS BOYS BOYS. They were in a bold white font against the fabric of a black T-shirt.

I noticed rainbow flags waving from the shops and restaurants. "What do those flags represent?" I asked Jochim naively. Jochim was a university student. He was a volunteer.

"It's the Gay Pride flag," Jochim explained to me as we walked down the cobbled streets of the old town. "Some people call Cologne the alternative gay capital of Europe."

It was rather brave of him to chauffeur a few dozen international high school aged students around Rudolfpltaz-Schaafenstrasse and Heumarkt-Mathiasstrasse. I took a picture of a sign with a phallus-shaped cactus.

"What does 'Puddelrüh durch die Prärie' mean in German?" I asked Jochim again.

"Don't worry about it," Jochim dismissed my question and continued walking.

Queerness was relatively absent from my upbringing. However, this might be a surprise for some people, but I am in fact not the first person to come out of the closet in my immediate family. This would be my 舅父 (kau⁵fu⁶; maternal uncle). Like me, my uncle was born in Te Awakairangi in a time when both Asian and Queer visibility in Aotearoa were slowly emerging from within the depths of the closet.

One of my most memorable encounters with my uncle was a family visit back in the late 1990s. I was incredibly young at the time, and I remember seeing his nails which were painted black. I was confused, but I was also curious as to why a boy would wear nail polish.

「我可唔可以油我指甲呀.」 (Can I paint my nails?) I asked Mum after he left.

「我畀你油.」 (I'll let you.) Mum laughed at my silly question. 「但係只可以油透明指甲油.」 (But you can only use the clear nail polish.)

Despite my uncle being out in most facets of his life, his sexuality was treated as an open secret by my family. My parents actively avoided talking about his relationships. This is because Queerness was seen as an undesirable trait. Queer behaviour was seen as an affront to Confucian values which emphasised the duty of children to continue the family line. Although homosexual behaviour was tolerated to an extent in traditional Cantonese society, there was still an expectation for children to be married with the sole purpose of providing heirs.

Added to this, Christian values condemning expressions of Queerness were embedded in the psyche of Hongkongers as a result of British colonisation. Christian missionaries from Europe came to civilise heathen cultures across Asia (Siker, 2006). This stemmed from conservative interpretations of the Bible which argued that Queer relationships were seen as unnatural and a chosen behaviour which could be changed. These latent discriminatory beliefs would end up infiltrating communities of the diaspora. We were warned as children to watch out for Queer people, described as 變態 (bin³taai³; mentally disturbed), who would prey on innocent children like me and my brother. The graphic 雞姦 (gai¹gaan¹; to bugger) was used to instil fear in children.

Both my brother and I were taught from a young age to identify Queer people based on their uncharacteristically gender non-conforming behaviour. Queer people were viewed as groomers and were to be avoided. Of course, these dangers posed by Queer people were likely as overstated and over-represented in the British colony as they have been globally. Queer-coded villains were mediated to us through the media in film and television, most notably in Disney productions such as Ursula in *The Little*

Mermaid (1989), Jafar in *Aladdin* (1992), and Scar in *The Lion King* (1994) to name a few.

Outside of mainstream white media, I was greatly influenced by Hong Kong media. It is through this media that I developed a number of unconscious biases about Queer people. We took monthly trips to the post office to collect boxes upon boxes of video tape recordings of unwanted television programmes and movies from our relatives in Hong Kong. This was in a time before satellite television and reliable internet connection.

In one crime show, the suspected murderer of a homicide case was a transgender woman, played by a cis female actor, who killed her wife in order to use the insurance pay out to medically transition. The main story arc focused on the authenticity and trustworthiness of the suspect and the motivations behind her transition. This made a deep impression on me, and it took me a long time to consciously unlearn harmful biases about our transgender communities.

If not the villain, then Queer people were often the butt of a joke as in the case of *The Iron Ladies* (2000). The film was based on the true events of the Iron Ladies who were a Thai volleyball team of mainly gay and transgender players. Slurs were used liberally throughout the film as a direct translation of the Thai word *kathoey*.

Despite the shortcomings of positive Queer representation in Hong Kong, films like *Rouge* 「胭脂扣」 (1988) provided me with the scaffold to develop my understanding of gender and sexuality within a Cantonese context. Both leads, Leslie Cheung 張國榮 and Anita Mui 梅艷芳, who were already known for their non-conforming expressions of gender in their music, challenged prevailing notions of gender and sexuality in pre-postcolonial Hong Kong. In the climax of the supernatural romantic drama film, Leslie's character makes love to Anita's character while she was presenting as a man. The significance of this scene became more apparent when he came out publicly as bisexual in 1992 where he said: "My mind is bisexual. It's easy for me to love a woman. It's also easy for me to love a man, too" (Chan, 2010).

My parents had no issues with me or my brother watching *Rouge* despite the Queer undertones. However, we were forbidden to watch Leslie's later films, such as *Farewell My Concubine* 「霸王別姬」 (1993) and *Happy Together* 「春光乍洩」 (1997), where Queerness was made more explicit.

As the adage goes, 「遠水不能救近火」 (water from afar cannot put out a nearby fire), the only role model I had in Aotearoa was my uncle. Beyond brief encounters at family gatherings, I never had the opportunity to connect with my uncle because of our generational divide. My uncle is a famous poet in Aotearoa. It will not take much to uncover his identity. I had not experienced his poetry until 2017. He was in Ōtautahi for a poetry reading and I went along with a doctoral student who knew my uncle. We were late for the event, so we snuck in quietly and found some seats at the back of the room. There I was, listening to him recite his poetry. He spoke so candidly about his sexuality and his Queerness. It was the first time I saw myself – a closeted Queer Asian in Aotearoa – represented in art.

My uncle does not know this, but he was my only family member to meet my long-distance come out boyfriend. We met when he was once again in Ōtautahi to present his poetry. I wanted to him there, but fear held me back. I never got the opportunity to come out to my uncle. It was not until recently when I published an online article that he reached out to me with words of support. He told me he was proud of me for sharing this part of my life with others and he hoped that my parents would eventually learn to accept me and my partner.

My uncle told me it took a long time, some tears, plenty of negotiation, and now plenty of talking to be at the stage he is at now with his parents. I often wonder how different my coming out experience would be if I had had my uncle by my side to guide me through my journey.

Self-exploration
Te Awakairangi, Summer 2012

I was unloading groceries from the car, when I heard an unusual amount of commotion from our normally quiet suburban street. I saw a group of teenage girls walking past the house.

"Go home to where you came from you fucking chink!" One girl shouted across the road. I looked around and I realised that they were talking about me.

"Why don't you just fuck off!" I retaliated with my best come back at the time.

The girls continued shouting insults and the chorus of abuse echoed through the street as they walked away.

"Homo!"

"Ching Chong!"

"Gaybo!"

I was speechless, but I was familiar with racist attacks. One time, I was lining up for the hydro slide at our local swimming pool. Another kid pushed past me before telling me to "go back to where you came from". I was only in primary school at the time.

But this time it was different. As I recalled the incident, I was flooded by a sense of dread. Why would they call me homo? Was there something particularly Queer about my appearance? I knew that deep down, I was different.

My parents were always open about human sexuality. They were never shy about the subject. I believe it is because they grew up during a period of rapid development and modernisation in Hong Kong, which is why they held relatively liberal views on sexuality. This was congruent with our Taoist beliefs where sex was a natural aspect of life. Startlingly, my parents did not hold similar liberal views about self-pleasure, as there were no benefits to this practice. Unnecessary seminal ejaculation was said to withdraw energy from the body. Furthermore, the Confucian belief system argued that non-procreative sexual behaviour was seen as an affront to filial piety.

The internet allowed me to explore my body and my feelings away from the watchful gaze of my parents. We got our first household computer when I was at intermediate school. This was when I was going through puberty, and I stumbled across a stock image website called the Banana Club. I would spend hours in front of my computer screen and scroll through thousands of images of naked men. I examined their physique, but I convinced myself that my feelings came from admiration as opposed to attraction.

The internet was not my only source of knowledge. The education system provided the foundation of my understanding around sexuality. We were taught about our changing bodies in health and physical education in intermediate school. We were shown images, videos, and sketches of how our body would change through puberty. One thing that was missing from these exemplars was that I did not see myself represented by the types of bodies shown in class.

"Boys will grow taller and gain greater muscle mass," the teacher told us matter-of-factly. "You will develop body and facial hair as you grow into men."

I looked at the other boys around me, largely Pākehā, who were already showing the hallmarks of masculinity. On the other hand, I was short in stature and my face, chest, and limbs were smooth and hairless. I looked nothing like the other boys around me.

"Was there something wrong with me?" I thought to myself as I watched the boys around me develop into men. "Will I ever be a man?"

I felt fortunate that I attended a secular co-educational school where sexual education was taught with little religious overtones. The teachers told us that sex between a man and a woman was a natural progression of human relationships. They taught us how to avoid unexpected pregnancies through contraception. They also described the horrors of sexually transmitted illnesses and diseases in extreme detail. The teachers rarely discussed diverse expressions of gender, sex, and sexuality in much detail, so I remained clueless on this aspect of identity. I slowly progressed to other explicit content on Tumblr, as I continued to explore my sexuality digitally. I spent hours trawling through images of naked men, but I convinced myself that my obsessive behaviour was a form of admiration. I did not want these men, but I wanted to be these men. As far as I was concerned, I was straight.

I only began thinking about what a relationship might look like for me in my senior years in high school when everyone was dating someone and everyone had to have a crush. I never understood why the boys in my class were only obsessed with girls.

"Is there something wrong with me for thinking about the boys at school as well?" I thought to myself as my eyes wandered and I fantasised about how I might get the attention of these boys.

"Sidney, you need to be careful," a classmate texted me one afternoon. "I heard a rumour that you're in love with Conrad."

Conrad was an exchange student from Germany. He was in my graphics and design class, and we were really close despite the language barrier.

"If you're not careful, Sidney," my classmate warned me. "People might think you're gay. You wouldn't want that, would you?"

After that warning, Conrad and I slowly drifted apart. In his final week in Aotearoa, he gifted me a *pounamu* (greenstone) necklace he bought in Tāhuna (Queenstown). It was a *roimata* (teardrop) which represents healing, comfort, and strength.

I spent the remainder of high school being cautious with my social interactions. I avoided interactions where my identity would come into question.

"I think I like you," a girl once told me on MSN Messenger. We went to the same high school, and she was a year below me.

"I think I like you too," I told her later on the phone. She was immensely popular, and I felt obliged to respond to her advances.

"I'm sorry, but we can't go out. My parents want me to focus on my studies," I told her much to her disappointment.

I would tell people this lie, repeatedly. It was much easier resorting to racial stereotypes than to confront the real reason why I did not want to be in a relationship.

Content warning

This chapter contains references to homophobia; mental illness and ableism; nudity; racism and racial slurs; self-harm and suicidal thoughts, intentions, and actions; substance use and abuse; and swear words or curse words.

The chapter starts overleaf.

3

to navigate the world alone

Ōtautahi, Summer 2013

After 18 years of living in Te Awakairangi, I was finally leaving my home. I was going to university. Little did my family know, this was the last time I would call Te Awakairangi my home as this was going to be my excuse to leave. The further away, the better. This was an opportunity for me to explore my identity on my own terms. This was one of the reasons why I chose the University of Canterbury in Ōtautahi (Christchurch). At the time, Ōtautahi was still recovering from the aftermath of the 2010–2011 Canterbury Earthquakes which devastated the region. The university offered generous scholarships to students to relocate to this city in ruins.

I could not have picked the worst day to leave. It was the second day of the Lunar New Year, when families would traditionally come together on this day to officially ring in the new year. Instead, we were heading to the airport to send me away. This occasion was not marked by a sense of liberation, but an omen of more difficult times to come. As we backed out of the driveway, we saw black paint splashed across the front of our house. We were the only house that had been targeted on the street. This mark was a physical reminder that we would never truly belong.

This sense of otherness followed me as I entered the loneliest period of my life. Most first-year university students typically stayed at a student residence. Since I could not afford to live at a residential hall, I shared an apartment with my high school friends, Andy and Jeff. Without realising it, I found myself in a "white closet".

Ōtautahi was known as "New Zealand's most English city" and the "most English of cities outside of England". Unfortunately, the city also held the reputation as "the most racist city in New Zealand". As I was surrounded by Pākehā people and spaces, I was expected to assimilate.

It was only once I left home that I learnt to appreciate what my parents constructed in Te Awakairangi. They created a home away from home where we could navigate our lives according to our Cantonese heritage. Now that I was by myself, I had to navigate the world differently. I was no longer free to express my culture without challenging whiteness.

"Go back to where you come from!" A group of teenage girls shouted at me while I was waiting at a bus stop. I was heading back to my flat from Northlands Mall.

I tried to ignore them until the bus arrived, but they followed me on to the bus. When they sat down, they threw rubbish at me while I sat with my back to them.

"Oi, fucking Asian!" the girls continued to abuse me.

The bus was partially full and no one, not even the driver, did anything to de-escalate the situation. They only stopped when I pretended to film them with my phone. When the group of girls finally got off the bus, they emptied their rubbish on my head.

They must have thought I was an easy target. I was feeling angry, sad, and hurt.

How naive could I be? I thought leaving Te Awakairangi would give me an opportunity to reinvent myself. The one thing I could not change was my racialised body.

An education
Ōtautahi, Autumn 2013

Outside of my flatmates, Andy and Jeff, I did not know anyone when I arrived in Ōtautahi. My social sphere stayed within the university, and I relied on my flatmates for human connection. The only exception to my social isolation were the few classmates from my speech and language pathology programme. I found it difficult to connect with my classmates due to the competitive nature of the programme.

On rare occasions, I would be invited to the odd student house party. The earthquakes flattened the city centre and the bars and hospitality scene virtually disappeared overnight. Our only options were house parties. With my limited social network, invitations to these parties were few and far between. However, it was at one of these house parties, where I had one of the most fruitful conversations in understanding my identity.

"We should go," Andy suggested.

I was at a house party with Andy and Jeff. Andy was in a long-distance relationship, and he had no interest in staying out late.

"Yeah, I'm done as well," Jeff agreed. He was also a homebody.

"Want to come with us to the Craic?" Cate and Sophie invited me. "It's karaoke night."

I was talking to Cate and Sophie who were two older students whom I met at the party. The Craic was a busy Irish bar on Riccarton Road. It was one of the few bars still standing near campus after the earthquakes.

"Lemme see," I told them. I looked at Andy and Jeff for validation.

Up until this point, Andy, Jeff, and I went everywhere together with the exception of class. I felt emotionally torn because I felt like I did not have a choice. It felt like they were my last connection to my childhood.

"Suit yourself," Sophie told me. She began making her way to the door. "We're going to meet our friend Joe. We'll see you there!"

"If you want to go just go. We'll just leave without you," Andy told me.

That was the permission I needed. I packed up my things and I made the journey to the Craic.

As I walked through the quiet streets of Riccarton, I was flooded with a sense of loneliness. I assumed when I moved in with my friends from high school that we would develop a stronger friendship. I felt like I was venturing into the unknown.

When I arrived at the Craic, I found Joe alone at the bar. He was nursing his beer watching the crowd sing and dance at the karaoke screen. I recognised him from the party earlier. Unluckily, for Joe, both Cate and Sophie had already left.

"You just missed them. They just left," Joe informed me. "Cate saw her ex outside."

"Would you like some company?" I asked Joe. I might as well stay.

Joe nodded and I went to get a drink and sat down next to him. We began to talk.

"I'm a fourth-year law and business student," Joe told me. "And I grew up in Lower Hutt.""Me too!" my eyes lit up. It was always nice discovering a point of common interest when meeting someone for the first time.

As we talked, I felt Joe's gaze drift from the crowd to me. He examined me from head to toe. First, he stroked my arm. Then my thigh. I pushed him away when he tried to kiss me.

"I'm sorry," Joe straightened himself up on the barstool. The mood of his tone shifted. "I just assumed you were family."

"No, it's fine." I was at a loss for words. "I'm just not ready to experiment."

I was both scared and surprised that Joe tried to kiss me. After four months attending student events and parties in Ōtautahi, I was used to being ignored and being invisible. I have never had someone express interest in me – so publicly.

"Are you gay?" I was curious.

"No, I'm bisexual," Joe replied without looking at me.

"What does that mean?" I asked innocently. I knew extraordinarily little about sexuality. "Let's get some fresh air," Joe told me. "I'll get us another drink."

Joe met me in the car park behind the Craic. This was meant to be a garden portion of the bar. He handed me a pint of beer before lighting up a cigarette.

"Do you smoke?" Joe asked me as he passed me the cigarette.

I took the cigarette and inhaled. I spluttered and choked on the foul smoke. I could taste the ash in my mouth. Within seconds, I felt light-headed and relaxed.

"How do I explain bisexuality?" Joe pondered for a moment.

"You know when you've had vanilla ice cream your whole life. And then suddenly you try chocolate ice cream?"

I nodded. I did not know where he was going with this analogy.

"Basically, vanilla ice cream was how I felt about women and chocolate ice cream was how I felt about men."

"I thought chocolate ice cream was the best thing in the world, but after having nothing but chocolate ice cream for I while, I wanted to go back to vanilla ice cream again."

"I realised I liked the taste of both women and men," Joe finished his story and took another drag of his cigarette.

I felt like I had reached a state of deep understanding about my own sexuality. All it took was someone to explain their feelings with plain language. The way Joe explained his sexuality was so simple yet logical.

I thought deeply about Joe's analogy, and I realised sexuality was a spectrum. I would later come to learn that for some people, it was possible to fall on either end of the spectrum or not on the spectrum at all.

"I always felt different growing up," Joe told me candidly.

Joe continued to describe his sexual encounters with other men in detail. I was in awe, but also mildly disturbed, although I understood his intentions. What was there to be disgusted about with human attraction?

"You've known, I've always had a thing for Asian men," Joe told me. I once again felt his gaze examining my body. "I think they're irresistible."

"Anyway, it's getting late," Joe announced as he stamped out his last cigarette. "I'll walk you home – if you'd like me to join you."

When I woke up the next day with a blaring headache, I thought my encounter from the night before was all a dream. I knew it was not a dream when I found a mobile number on a sheet of paper and an unopened condom in my pocket. Joe had handed them to me outside my flat as we parted ways. Perhaps I was ready to experiment with my sexuality after all.

Incognito mode
Ōtautahi, Spring 2013

While I learnt to navigate the white closet constructed around me as a racialised person, I found myself enclosed within another closet – one I tried to suppress. I only had a latent understanding of my Queerness. Even though I watched gay porn, I did not think there was anything unusual about it. As long as no one knew about this, I considered myself straight. I was only meant to be attracted to women after all. I distanced myself from Queerness – both people and spaces – to steer myself away from difficult questions.

"I wonder why we always end up with women and gays in speech therapy," Emma proclaimed loudly to the group.

"Well, I'm not gay," I whispered quietly to myself. There was a running joke in my class that straight men were not interested in studying speech and language pathology.

"What I was going to say," Emma never finished her sentence as we boarded the bus.

It was Guy Fawkes Night. Every year the city council would host a large public display by New Brighton beach. We went as a cohort, and we were just heading home from the event. The bus heading back to the city was packed. As we waited for the traffic to clear, I noticed everyone was whispering and pointing at the two men on the bus.

"Oh my God, what the fuck are they doing?" Emma whispered in shock.

There were two men standing by the back door. One of them was holding on to a guard-rail of the bus, while the other had his arms around him. The one holding on to the guard rail was making a stroking motion. I was intrigued to know what these two were doing to cause such a commotion. From certain angles on the bus, it looked like one of the men was getting a hand-job. No wonder they were the centre of attention. Not only was it a public display of Queer affection, but it also looked like they were pleasuring each other in public. As I watched the two men, I realised I knew one of the two men. Elliot was a friend of mine.

"Hey Sidney!" Elliot must have felt me staring at the bus and greeted me.

As Elliot waved to me at the back of the bus, I looked away. I did not know why, but I felt a deep sense of shame when Elliot acknowledged our connection. I did not want to be Queer by association.

"Is that your friend?" Emma demanded to know.

"No," I lied and slunk into the shadows.

When Elliot saw me ignore him, he stopped waving. He must have realised something was wrong. Elliot and his companion got off the bus not long afterwards.

A few days later, I received an unexpected message from Elliot.

"I just wanted to apologise for the other day," Elliot told me. "I've been meaning to message you. I shouldn't have spoken to you in such a situation. Sorry about that."

"You don't need to apologise. I was more taken aback by the situation," I finally responded to Elliot after some time. "I didn't know how to respond to what happened. If you want, we can meet up some time."

A small part of me wanted him to give me more details. "Was he your boyfriend?" "How long have you been dating?" "When did you know when you were gay?" "Do you think I'm gay?" I kept those questions to myself.

"I wanted to message you about that night, but I didn't think I was in a position to ask for an explanation," I continued.

"It's okay; I didn't mean to put you in that situation. I'm not sure what there was to explain. You can ask me anything if there's something you're not sure about," Elliot seemed confused with my reaction to this insignificant event.

"No, that's fine. I won't bring it up with our friends," I continued spiralling.

"Okay, thanks. I'm not sure what it is. I just felt bad for putting you into an awkward situation." "I'll keep it a secret," I reassured Elliot again. Our conversation was going around in circles. "Keep what a secret? I'm rather confused as to what needs to be kept secretive?"

I let the conversation peter out. Elliot was rightfully confused as I was not sure what the secret was either. Maybe I thought I was doing Elliot favour by not outing him to his friends. He was already out to his family and friends, so what was there to protect? Perhaps I wanted him to keep my secret instead.

Quake city
Ōtautahi, Spring 2013

It was coming to the end of my first year at university. Even though my social life was non-existent, I excelled academically. I was offered a place on the professional programme for speech and language pathology. However, there were a few changes to my living situation. Andy decided to return home to Te Awakairangi to join his girlfriend, and Jeff decided to move in with his girlfriend. I was once again alone.

With the prospect of moving into a new flat, I moved in with a friend Ella who also lived in the same apartment complex. The new apartment was a lot more expensive, so I applied for any job I could find as I was running low on funds. There was an entry-level role processing earthquake claims at a private insurance company. Much of the city centre was still in ruins and the residential areas were still in disrepair.

I still remember the day of the interview. It was a warm day. The Nor 'wester was in full force – a strong hot and humid north-westerly wind. This was the day I met Thomas. He was the first friend I made in Ōtautahi. What sparked this unlikely friendship was another case of fateful coincidence. Thomas was also at the interview for this entry-level role. I took my time heading home after the interview. Unknowingly, Thomas appeared next to me at the bus stop.

"Nice to meet you, I'm Sidney," I introduced myself to the stranger. I recognised him from the interview. "Are you applying for the same role?"

"Yes, I am," Thomas responded hesitantly. "I'm Thomas, by the way."

"Are you taking the Orbiter? Mind if I join you?" I asked hoping for some company.

Thomas nodded and gestured for me to sit next to him at the bus stop. I am not normally one to talk to strangers, but something prompted me to introduce myself to him. He is Pākehā and he grew up just north of Ōtautahi. At that time, he was a third-year law student. As we continued talking on the bus, I found out he was living in the apartment building next to mine.

"Should we get a drink at the Foundry?" I suggested.

"Sure. I've got nothing else planned," Thomas replied eagerly.

Thomas and I got off the bus and we made our way to the Foundry – the student bar. Even though we only shared a jug of beer, we lost track of time as we raced through a range of topics that afternoon. We learnt so much about each other such as our interests, our differences, and our similarities. If I had known better, this could have been our first date.

While Thomas and I waited for the results from the interview, we stayed connected. Thankfully, we were both offered a position. On the one hand, I was excited we were going to spend the summer together. On the other hand, I had to break the news to my parents. Both my parents were expecting me to go home that summer as my brother had done after his first year at university. I was not going home, to their disappointment.

「你諗唔諗住返屋企架.」 (Are you coming home?) Mum asked me one afternoon.

「唔返啦，我搵到份工.」 (I'm not coming home; I found a job.) I told her.

「哦，咁呀。記得睇住自己啦.」 (Oh, is that so, just look after yourself then.) Mum seemed disappointed.

Before Thomas and I began our role at the private insurance company, we spent a lot of time together running errands. The first time we spent time together alone, we drove a short distance from the city. We walked around a remote suburb to get some fresh air away from exam study. We sat outside the dairy overlooking the tall grass. We talked some more about our past and our aspirations. It felt like we were dating, and I was beginning to develop feelings for him.

As our friendship progressed, I began to worry I was getting too clingy. Although I enjoyed spending my time talking to Thomas, I was worried I was becoming overly dependent on him as a friend. When Thomas and I started our role at the insurance company, I kept my distance from him to give him some space. I did not want to come across as too possessive.

"Want to get a beer?" I asked Thomas after an unproductive day at work.

Thomas nodded enthusiastically. I could tell he had had a tough week.

When Thomas and I got back to his apartment, we began to drink. One beer became two. Two beers became three. Once the beer was finished, we started to drink whisky. He brought out the cigars he had hidden in his room. The more we drank, the more vulnerable we became. We became quite emotional as we shared our most intimate thoughts.

"You know, life really sucks when you're different. I was a loner at high school," Thomas told me. He took a puff of his cigar and passed it to me. "I've never felt a sense of attachment."

"I know what you mean," I replied. "I don't know how to maintain friends. I struggle to know what people want. I feel like a people pleaser."

"Really? I thought only I felt that way," Thomas reacted with surprise. "You know, I once tried to end it all. It thought like an easy way out of this mess. The only thing that stopped me from following through with it was that I didn't how to do it."

When Thomas and I finished the cigar, I went back to my apartment. On my way home, I sat down on a fence. I needed a moment alone to process my thoughts. I started sobbing. It dawned on me how much pain there was in the world. I also realised how miserable I was in Ōtautahi. I was alone and I was exhausted from hiding in the white closet.

Most of my life, I had been preoccupied with what other people thought of me. Whether it was family, friends, or strangers, I always pandered for their affection to get a sense of validation. Now that I was alone in a city that had no love for me, I no longer knew what my purpose was in the world. I wondered briefly, what I could do to get out of this mess, before coming back to my senses. I recognised that for me to move on I would need to come to terms with my past before I could move on to the next stage of my life.

Content warning

This chapter contains references to body hatred and fatphobia; death, dying, and mass murder; homophobia; mental illness and ableism; nudity; racism and racial slurs; substance use and abuse; and sexual assault.

The chapter starts overleaf.

4
to obtain enlightenment

Ōtautahi, Summer 2014

I was in my second year at university. At this point, I had dropped out of the speech and language pathology programme. I had transferred to a science degree in linguistics instead. I told my course co-ordinators that I wanted to pursue my interest in linguistics. I spent days deliberating with my flatmate Ella as to whether I should make the change. In all honesty, I was sick of the homophobic remarks from other students. I did not want to question my sexuality anymore.

I was still in my part-time role settling earthquake claims. Our contracts were extended from three months to twelve months. I still struggled with the white closet, but I enjoyed my time at the insurance company more than my time at the university.

I expanded my social circle beyond the university with my connections at the insurance company. I worked hard settling claims and I was popular with the full-time staff. I also had Thomas by my side, even though our relationship remained platonic. I only found out years later that he was attracted to me after we spent a night together. Sometimes the right person comes into your life at the wrong time. If only I had come out to myself when we met.

My tasks were mind-numbing at best, but management tried their best to make the work tolerable. It was their prerogative to settle the claims as soon as feasibly possible as it was a drain on their resources. One of my main tasks was to collect insurance excesses from homeowners. What was meant to be a straightforward task would often be an emotionally bruising experience.

The people I spoke to would recount their trauma, which had been caused by the natural disaster. They would break down in tears as they talked about loved ones who had been killed in the earthquake. I still vividly remember a woman blaming me for the death of her grandchild who died in one of the events. My foreign-sounding last name made it extra difficult for me to connect with the homeowners as they assumed that I was located in an offshore call centre. My only redeeming feature was my white accent.

Management recognised the emotional toll in this earthquake space, so we were often offered treats and rewards. We had a trolley of savouries and scones that would make its way through the building every morning. On Fridays, the mail trolley would be replaced with beer and wine. I had no choice as I was still a student, and I needed the money.

There was no competition in the office. Between the gentle tap-tapping of keyboards and clicking between archaic software, I had some of my most honest conversations while I was working at the insurance company.

"Our lives would be so much easier if we were white," Lucette announced loudly.

It was a quiet Saturday morning in the office. Lucette and I were processing loss adjustment payments. No one else wanted to do overtime with us on a Saturday morning. Lucette is South African Indian and migrated to Ōtautahi with her family.

"Sometimes I wish I wasn't Asian," She continued. "If I was white, I wouldn't have to deal with all this racist shit."

I nodded in agreement. Lucette and I were talking about our experiences of racism in Ōtautahi. Just a few weeks earlier, I was at a supermarket with another colleague when a Pākehā man with a shaved head shoved me against the supermarket shelf and told me to "Go back to where you come from, Asian cunt!"

Lucette realised much earlier than I did that our racialised bodies were not welcome in Ōtautahi. Ironically, her family left South Africa to escape institutional racism only to settle in the "white supremacist capital of New Zealand".

"I'd still rather be doing this than being in South Africa," Lucette shrugged and continued to process the payments.

I felt a sense of comfort talking to Lucette who understood what it meant to be a racialised person in Aotearoa. When I shared my experiences of racism in Ōtautahi with her, I briefly felt visible in this white closet.

Sudden realisation
Ōtautahi, Spring 2014

As I continued to work at the insurance company, my social life flourished while my academic aspirations stagnated. Before long, I was invited to a colleague's birthday party. She held her fiftieth birthday party at her home. It was a cool spring evening, and the smell of dew hung in the air. I knew no one at the party, so I found myself alone drinking in her garden.

I was lost in my thoughts when Iain stumbled into the garden. I recognised Iain from another party a few weeks earlier. He had left the insurance company before I started, but I knew that he was openly gay through the grapevine. When we made eye contact, Iain made his way towards me. Little did I know that this was going to another fateful coincidence that would propel me on my journey of self-discovery.

"Hey," Iain greeted me. He tripped over himself.

"Hey," I replied casually.

I stood there in the yard feeling cold, drunk, and lost in thought. Iain was visibly drunk, but he did not repulse me. Iain had a small frame, and he was no taller than I was. He was an extremely attractive man with handsome features.

"Have you ever kissed a boy?" Iain asked me.

"No, I haven't," I answered anxiously.

"Do you want to kiss a boy?" Iain teased me.

"I don't know," I whispered my reply.

"How would you know if you've never tried?" Iain whispered in return.

Before my mind could comprehend what was happening, Iain had already wrapped his arms around my body and pulled me into him. We locked our bodies in a tight embrace and our lips touched. I was breathless. As we kissed, time stood still, and I forgot where we were. I knew in that moment that my life would never be the same. I felt enlightened. This one kiss brought to the surface my hidden desires. I wanted more. I had just unlocked a new milestone in my life.

When I noticed people watching Iain and me through the window, I pushed him away. Even though I did not want that moment to stop, fear brought me back to my senses. As I left Iain alone in the garden, I tried to process what had just happened to me. A part of me wanted that kiss to last forever, while another part of me feared for what the future had in store for me. I was both elated and disgusted by how much I enjoyed the kiss. I was an emotional wreck.

I stumbled away from the party towards the street. I sat myself down on a neighbour's fence to process the events of the evening. After what felt like a lifetime alone with my thoughts, I heard someone approaching. I saw Iain once again stumbling towards me.

"Want to come home with me?" Iain offered his drunken proposition.

I shook my head. One kiss was more than enough for the night. Iain stumbled away from me and disappeared into the night.

"Let's get you home," my colleague gestured towards her car.

When I finally got back to the apartment, I crawled up the four flights of stairs to my apartment. I knocked on Ella's door.

"Are you okay?" Ella asked me. She cautiously opened her door.

"I think there is something wrong with me?" I responded to Ella with another question before collapsing on the floor.

"No, of course not," Ella replied and laid down next to me.

I recalled the events of the evening to Ella. I told her about my conversation with Joe and my kiss with Iain. She was the first person I came out to about my sexual desires.

"I know how you're feeling," Ella tried to comfort me with her words.

Ella confided in me and told me about her bisexuality. She was also going on her own journey to understand what that meant to her. I felt a sense of comfort lying on the carpet.

After listening to Ella, I went back to my room. I was still drunk at this point, and I began overanalysing the situation. I could not sleep so I called Joe instead.

"Can I talk to you about something?" I asked Joe. "Sure, man," Joe managed in reply. "Are you okay?"

I made my way to Joe's flat. When I arrived, he was waiting for me outside on the driveway. He was barefoot and in his pyjamas. He offered me a beer before he led me to his room. Joe lit a cigarette as I recalled the events of the evening.

Forbidden knowledge
Ōtautahi, Spring 2014

I was hyper-fixated on that moment for the next several weeks. Within days, I started searching for resources to help me understand my feelings. I went online and trawled through websites and blogs. I then went to the university library to find books about sexuality to frame my identity within an academic framework. Perhaps it would make it easier to except myself if there was a scientific basis to my behaviour. I was nervous strangers would see my reading material, so I wedged them between other books to smuggle them out of the library.

It was also during this time that I was introduced to RuPaul's Drag Race. I first saw a video a gay colleague shared on their Facebook feed, and I was intrigued with the diverse range of drag artists. I pirated a season from the internet, and I watched the episodes in my room behind locked doors. I had no idea that a whole Queer subculture existed.

Even though I had found some resources to distract me, I still could not shake off the memory of that night. When I kissed Iain, I finally saw the part of my life I had spent in denial. Suddenly, everything made sense. For the first time in my life, I saw my life with some sense of clarity. I knew I had to speak to Iain, so I found Iain on Facebook, and it took me a week before I finally built up the courage to send him a message.

"This is a bit awkward to talk about at 8:30 in the morning, eh?" I joked.

"Oh, shit! Sorry about what happened," Iain replied after seeing my message.

I had no idea why he was apologising.

"I want to talk about it, but I don't want to make you feel awkward," I replied anxiously. "Of course, same here, I didn't realise that story got around that fast."

It did not take long before our kiss reached the office. I was worried what people might say about us, but it also felt nice to be the centre of attention.

"I'm not usually like this," I confessed to Iain.

"Same, it's been a bit crazy since I came out," Iain replied.

I did not realise that he had only just come out. I just assumed that those who had the courage to be themselves in public were always out.

"So, do you like men? Women? Both?" I asked curiously.

"I was with a girl for four years and I thought I was bisexual, but I am into guys for sure," Iain responded with certainty.

I took some time to think about what I was going to say next.

"Do you feel comfortable talking about this?" I asked to clarify.

"I've had two solid months of talking about it and coming out. So yes, I am. Well, take your time. There's no point rushing it. I'm what, late twenties? A bit late, but just shows it can be tricky," Iain replied candidly.

I was surprised. I thought I was the only one exploring my sexuality this late in life.

"The thing is I enjoyed our kiss. I'm not sure how to process that part," I confessed to Iain. "Oh really. I didn't expect you to enjoy it. I thought I might've scared you."

Iain seemed surprised. It must be because I told him I did not want to go home with him.

"I wouldn't be talking to you if I was scared," I reassured Iain.

"Well, that's cool. I can't tell you what it means for you, but I know in my experience I kind of knew for ages but denied it. It depends," Iain paused for a few seconds and continued. "I'm sorry, I just mean I can't decide or process what happened for you. It's all experience really. A hook up here and there is okay. You learnt something out of it."

"If you're keen, do you want to meet up sometime?" I asked Iain.

"Sure man, I'm happy to talk about it," Iain replied. "It will get inside your head a bit."

Like a crack in a dam, the walls surrounding my closet began to break down. Slowly but steadily, a stream of uncontrollable events occurred one after the other. I had many questions, and I wanted to understand what was going on inside my mind. Iain and I met for lunch the following day. I was extremely nervous leading up to our meeting.

"My parents are from South Africa, but they moved to Gisborne," Iain told me.

We talked for hours over lunch. Iain told me about his past relationships and his family's reaction to his coming out. When I spoke to Iain, I felt a sense of comfort.

"We're going to work together by the way," Iain told me excitedly as we finally left the restaurant. "I start next week. See you there!"

Iain inspired me to go on a journey of self-discovery. It felt like everything that was happening from this point in my life was outside my control. If it were not for our fateful coincidence, my life would have headed in a different trajectory.

Unfortunately, my friendship with Joe deteriorated. Outside of Thomas, he was my only other friend. There was a sudden shift in our relationship dynamic after I told him about my kiss.

"Can I light up in here?" Joe asked me one evening.

Joe was sitting on my bed. I knew it was rhetorical. My apartment had a strict no smoking policy, but I was not sober enough to care.

I was not sure how Joe made it to my room. All I could remember was that he called me earlier that afternoon before he invited himself over to my flat. He was unexpectedly insistent.

Joe lit a cigarette and began inspecting my body through the veil of smoke. I was no longer just a friend; I became an object of desire.

"Well, do you want to see my dick?" Joe asked me.

"What?" I was astonished by his question.

Joe stood up and unbuckled himself. He pushed me against the bed. All I could remember next was the smell of cigarette smoke. The ashen stench hung in the air of my room. I felt dirty. I thought he was someone in whom I could confide. I have not spoken to Joe since that afternoon.

Impulsive Decisions
Ōtautahi, Summer 2014

"We need more full-timers," our operations manager announced one afternoon.

It had been four years since the devastating earthquakes, and the number of over cap claims kept increasing. The company needed more consultants to settle the increasing number of complex earthquake claims. I had been working at the company for nearly two years by then. I was content with my part-time position, and I had become close friends with my colleagues.

"Are you going to apply?" Iain asked me one afternoon.

"I don't know," I replied unconvincingly.

The university was about to break for the summer, and I was going to return in the new year to finish my degree. I wanted to leave Ōtautahi as soon as I could.

A few days after the announcement, the operations manager sent out an email announcing the new team of senior consultants. One of them was Iain.

"I got the role," Iain told me excitedly from his cubicle.

I smiled at Iain and gave him a double thumbs up from my desk. I felt a knot developing in my throat and a sinking feeling in my stomach. Even though we were just friends, I had developed romantic feelings for Iain since our first kiss. I realised that I would no longer be in the same team as Iain. I was going to miss my one opportunity to be closer to Iain. I stood up from my cubicle and I walked hurriedly towards my manager. I felt my heart beating loudly in my chest as I knew that what I was about to do next was impulsive.

"Could I please have a quick word with you?" I whispered to my manager. "Sure thing," my manager replied. "Do we need to go somewhere private?"

"Yes please," I told him as we walked into a meeting room. "Is it too late for me to apply?" "Of course not," my manager winked at me. "We still have to go through the usual process."

They offered me the senior role within two days. I immediately unenrolled from university.

"Are you sure this is a good idea?" Thomas asked me when I told him about my new appointment. He knew about my feelings for Iain. He seemed upset with my news.

"Why wouldn't this be a good idea?" I asked Thomas with genuine curiosity.

"Just make sure you are doing this for you, and not for anyone else," Thomas interjected before returning to processing his loss adjustment payments.

With a stroke of good luck, I was placed in Iain's team. The two of us were inseparable. We shared a cubicle, and we constantly messaged each other. He introduced me to his friends, and we went to the same parties.

After working together for a month, my wildest dream finally came true. Iain and I had been at a party earlier that afternoon and we had decided to go for a walk to get more drinks, but we ended up sitting in the car park of the Bush Inn Centre not far from my flat.

Iain and I opened up the box of cider and he passed me a menthol cigarette. We were on our backs watching the stars above us.

"I need you to know something, Sid," Iain confessed to me as he sat up. The moonlight illuminated the asphalt around us. "I've liked you since I first met you at Margaret's party."

"I couldn't believe my luck when you ended up in my team," Iain confessed.

Iain leant in towards me and we kissed. Once again, time stood still.

"I like you, too," I whispered to Iain under my breath. "Do you want to go home with me?"

I took Iain back to my flat and we spent the night together. Not long after our second kiss in the car park, we were dating.

I was still in the closet, and I was not ready to come out at work. During the day, we pretended to be best friends, and at night, he would meet me at my flat. In the morning, we would go to work separately. This became our routine.

Despite both of us coming out at the same time, Iain was a lot more in touch with his body than I was with mine. I struggled with my body image, and I was not comfortable seeing my naked body or expressing pleasure during sex.

It did not take long for people at work to suspect there was something between Iain and me. It did not bother me as I realised, eventually, that we would need to come clean with our relationship.

"We know you two are together," a colleague told Iain and me in a meeting room one day. "Don't worry, I won't tell anyone."

I felt as though I was on course to coming out as long as Iain was there by my side.

Nevertheless, some romances were not meant to last. As the weeks progressed, Iain grew distant. Our daily meetings became less frequent. After a lonely weekend, I did not see him at work on Monday morning.

"Where's Iain?" a colleague asked me. "I haven't heard from him all weekend."

"I don't know," I shrugged. I was as confused as they were. I had sent Iain multiple text messages over the course of the weekend but had had no replies.

"Iain?" our team manager piped up over the cubicle wall. "He was in a wee incident with his scooter. He'll be back in a few days."

"Are you okay? I'm coming over to yours," I told Iain on the phone. "I don't care if you don't want to see me. We need to talk."

I took the bus to his flat and he greeted me at the door. I handed him a care package before going in – inside was homemade chicken sweet corn soup and some chocolate.

"I was drinking with a guy I was kind of seeing before we started dating," Iain admitted to me. "I swear nothing happened between us, but I got a bit drunk and fell off my scooter. I'm sorry; I think we're better off as friends."

Our romance had lasted the summer, and by autumn, I was once again alone.

Content warning

This chapter contains references to body hatred and fat phobia; homophobia; mental illness and ableism; nudity; racism and racial slurs; substance use and abuse; transphobia; and violence.

The chapter starts overleaf.

5
to obsess without reason

Rotorua, Summer 2015

After my brief relationship with Iain, I once again felt alone and lost. I felt like I had nothing left. I was no longer studying towards my degree, and I was working in an unsatisfying job. I had no reason to be in Ōtautahi. I was loveless in what felt like a loveless city.

Thankfully, I had already planned a temporary escape from Ōtautahi.

"Would you like to show me around New Zealand?" Jochim had messaged me on Facebook a few months earlier. The same Jochim who took me around the old town of Cologne.

Jochim and his friend, Lotte, were geography students. They had a conference in Australia and had decided to come to Aotearoa for a week. He invited his friend Menno to join us. We hired a motor home, and we spent the week travelling around Te Ika-a-Maui (the North Island).

While we were in Rotorua, Jochim and Lotte ended up in an intense argument. They had been childhood friends. After a fast volley of German, Jochim stormed out of the motor home. Lotte ran out of the motor home shortly after.

"What should we do?" I asked Menno as we exchanged uncomfortable looks at each other. I was in a state of confusion. My beginner's German did not give me the vocabulary to understand the content of their argument.

"We could go find them," Menno suggested. "Or we could get drunk instead."

A sensible choice.

Menno found two wine glasses in the kitchenette, and he poured me a glass of red wine. We laid there on the mattress waiting for time to pass. Up until this point in the trip, we had not spoken to each other. Menno rested his head on his hand and smiled at me.

"Well," Menno asked as he slowly inched towards me. "Have you ever kissed a boy?" "H-how … how did you know?" I asked with concern. I was still learning about my sexuality.

I thought I did a good job masking my Queerness.

"I didn't know," Menno smirked and took another drink of his wine. Menno looked out of the window into the dense bush.

"How about you? Have you kissed I boy?" I asked Menno in return. It was only fair that he also volunteered this information.

"Many," Menno laughed. "Did Jochim not tell you I'm gay?"

"When did you know you were gay?" I asked curiously. Menno had my full attention.

"I don't know when I realised I was gay," Menno confessed. He threw his hands in the air and laughed. "I just knew I liked boys."

Menno stopped laughing and gently placed his hand on my shoulder. He looked me directly in the eyes.

"May I kiss you?" Menno requested.

"Yes," I obliged.

Our lips made contact and once again time came to a complete stop as I savoured the taste of red wine on his lips.

Slam. Jochim and Lotte returned to the motor home without warning. I began to realise some of the most memorable moments in life were also the shortest moments.

Over the course of that week, Menno became my guide. He was the living encyclopaedia to my ever-increasing list of questions about who I was to become.

"Who was your first kiss?"

"How was your first time?"

"When did you first come out?"

"How did your parents react to your sexuality?"

Nothing more developed from the brief kiss we shared in Rotorua. There were some tender moments when he embraced me in bed as we listened to the sound of waves crashing against the shores of Parawai (Thames) or while we briefly held hands as we walked down the pier of Tauranga Moana (Tauranga). My feelings for Menno departed with him when he left Aotearoa after that fateful week.

Finding space
Ōtautahi, Spring 2015

I had come out to myself and had come to terms with my Queerness, but I still kept my Queer identity hidden from my friends with the exception of a few key individuals like Erin.

As I began exploring my sexuality, I tried to connect with the visibly Queer people I knew – in most cases, unsuccessfully inserting myself into spaces that were either unsafe or where I was not welcome. I found that my greatest struggle at the time was trying to find a sense of belonging in this community. Queer spaces were virtually all destroyed by the earthquakes.

One of the only Queer spaces still standing was a self-styled gay bar called Cruz. Our Queer communities actively avoided this bar because it was well-known to be an unsafe space. As recently as 2019, the owner of Cruz posted transphobic messaging on an outdoor sign (Broughton, 2019). Other unverified rumours about the owner's behaviour were his preference for white twinks. The owner systematically removed patrons who did not fit into this narrow mould. One of my most vivid memories was when the owner kicked me out of the bar for "stealing" water.

"You're stealing!" The owner shouted as he stormed down from the DJ booth.

"Get him the fuck out of here!" He grabbed my arm and threw me towards the bouncer.

"It was only water," I confessed to the bouncer.

"I know," he told me. "The owner's a dick, but what can we do?"

It turned out I was not the first person to be kicked out for stealing water (Sachdeva, 2013). It was likely because I was not his preferred "type" of customer – if only I was slender and white. The only other physical Queer space was the sex cafe called Menfriends on Tuam Street. Again, another unsafe space for our Queer communities. As recently as 2018, the owners of Menfriends hosted an event, which specified only cisgender men could attend (Stuff, 2018). Some of the worst harm to our Queer communities comes directly from within our own communities.

I also learnt about cruising where men would wander public spaces with the aim of having anonymous sex. Of course, cruising is risky and can lead to unsafe sex. Some cruising sites include Hagley Park, Latimer Square, and Victoria Park. I have never actively been cruising, but I once spent some intimate time with a stranger who noticed me on Riccarton Road. This brief encounter did not last long when the stranger realised that his partner was watching him.

With physical spaces unavailable to me, the only feasible alternative was private house parties in Ōtautahi. The invites to these parties were deeply guarded secrets in a time when Queer spaces were scarce. Public events hosted by Christchurch Pride were yet to begin for another few years. With no direction, I tried to connect with Harvey to access these spaces. He was the only openly gay student in my class. We were close during our first year. Nevertheless, we drifted apart once I left the speech and language pathology programme. Perhaps our mutual Queerness would reconcile our friendship.

"Are you up to much?" I asked in a text message to Harvey after work on a Friday.

It was Halloween – also known as "Gay Christmas". Earlier in the week Harvey had mentioned that he was going to go to a Halloween party. It was unclear from his tone whether it was an open invite. I hoped he would introduce me to other Queer people in Ōtautahi.

"I'm at the party in Merivale," Harvey replied. "There's heaps of gays here."

"Sounds great, can I come?" I asked curiously.

"I'll ask," Harvey wrote back shortly afterwards.

While I waited for Harvey to reply, I started drinking alone at home. I was already slightly tipsy from the after-work drinks. I dressed as the character Russell from the movie *Up* (2009). My inspiration for the costume came from the leftover helium balloons at an office function. I generally hated fancy dress, so I normally put minimal effort into my costumes. I always felt uncomfortable pretending to be someone I was not.

With no new updates from Harvey, I went to another Halloween party. I checked my phone frequently, anticipating a reply, but I still did not hear from him. It was getting late, and my transport options were limited. If I delayed any longer, I would not be able to go at all. I decided to make my way towards the general direction of the party with the hope that Harvey would extend an invite to me. I struggled to get all my helium balloons into the bus. I knew that I was behaving irrationally. I was desperate to meet other Queer people and I was willing to do whatever it took.

"Where's the party?" I asked Harvey as I got off the bus.

I had finally decided to call Harvey after not hearing from him the whole night.

"Honestly, it'd be better if you didn't come," Harvey told me and hung up.

"Fuck," I thought to myself.

It was nearly midnight, and I was stuck in Merivale with no way home. I waited in the lobby of the McDonald's. Ella had told me once that Elliot lived nearby. The last time I had spoken to him was after Guy Fawkes Night. I was still avoiding him because I was worried people would associate me with his behaviour that night, but I was desperate.

"Can I crash at yours tonight?" I asked Elliot. "I've got no way to get home."

"That's fine, I'll meet you outside," Elliot responded sleepily. I was drunk and I was making irresponsible choices. Ironically, the person I was actively avoiding was also the only person who was willing to give me a safe space. Elliot greeted me at the gate.

"You can crash on the couch," Elliot offered generously. "Or you can sleep in my bed."

I was tipsy and too upset from the night's events to decide. My words were incoherent. Elliot led me to his room, and he tucked me into his bed.

"It's fine, we're just friends," Elliot comforted me.

Elliot hugged me from behind. He held me close to his body and I felt his penis press against my thigh. I instinctively pushed him away, and I shuffled to my side of the bed.

"You know friends can cuddle too, right?" Elliot teased. "It's not all about sex."

I was nervous, but I eventually surrendered my body to Elliot. He once again held me close to his body. Silence gave way to heavy breathing. I fell asleep in his embrace. I was finally in a safe space.

Submissive bodies
Ōtautahi, Spring 2015

With safe physical and virtual spaces ruled out, my last hope was the university wine club, which incidentally had a high concentration of attendees from our Queer communities. Even though this was a university club, most of the attendees were not students.

There were not a lot of activities in Ōtautahi after the earthquakes, and events like the wine club were one of a few outlets for people to socialise. After weeks of deliberation, I went along with Ella who was a regular attendee of their events. I wanted to meet other Queer people, but I did not have the courage to go by myself.

I met Bradley at my first university wine club. He was sitting across from me at the tasting table. We exchanged a few looks before I went back to my wine. At first, I was too shy to talk to him, but one glass of Riesling led to another, and we started to talk.

"Would you like to give me a hand with this fine bottle of wine?" I asked Bradley as the event ended. I was lucky enough to win a bottle of Riesling in the raffle.

"It'd be silly for me not to," Bradley joked.

We were all tipsy at this point. Bradley accompanied Ella and me as we walked back to our apartment on the other side of the university campus. We picked up another bottle of wine from the supermarket and we made ourselves comfortable in the common area.

Bradley was smart and charismatic. He told us about his work with his *iwi* (tribe). Ella sat there feeling very much like a third wheel.

"I'm going to bed," Ella announced around midnight. "Will you be okay, Sidney?"

"I'll be fine," I promised Ella. "I'll go to bed soon."

When Ella retired to her room down the hall, Bradley shuffled next to me on the couch. We once again exchanged looks like we had earlier that evening, but this time with greater intensity.

I do not remember how Bradley and I ended up alone in my room. I do remember the moment when he held me by my waist. He pulled me close to his body and kissed me on the lips. Bradley's lips moved down to my neck. When he softly bit the soft skin of my neck, I lost full control of my body. I knew whom I wanted, and he was with me in that moment.

Shiraz. Pinot Noir. Gewurztraminer. Over the course of the next few wine tastings, Bradley would come home with me. This became our routine.

Bradley took his time with me and never advanced beyond my levels of comfort. I figured it had to be his background in law – after all, consent is compulsory.

"Are you okay?" Bradley would ask. "We can take it slowly."

In every session, Bradley taught me a little bit more about my body. He also taught me an important lesson about safe sex – something I clearly had missed at school.

"Do you have a condom?" Bradley asked me one night.

"No," I replied innocently. "Why is that?"

"You must use a condom to keep yourself safe," Bradley told me as he got up from the bed. He removed a condom from his wallet and tore the silver packet open with his teeth.

"You should also get tested regularly," Bradley continued to lecture.

Bradley was kind, but I never felt like I was in control. The random glimpses of my naked body felt foreign to me. I continued to struggle with feeling pleasure.

"Can I top you?" I asked Bradley one evening.

"No," Bradley responded coldly. He seemed offended. "That's not how it works."

I realised in that moment that Bradley's patience was only an attempt to access my body. Asian men were meant to be submissive – another vestige of colonisation, where the bodies of Asian men were perceived as soft and effeminate. Our routine did not last long after that interaction.

From the margins
Ōtautahi, Spring 2015

With the absence of physical spaces in Ōtautahi, I retreated to virtual spaces. I downloaded Grindr and Tinder on my phone and began the hard lesson of navigating these transgressive spaces.

I learnt a new register of the English language specific to our gay communities. On these platforms, I encountered new concepts like twinks, bears, and otters. A twink was a young,boyish gay man. A bear was an older hairy gay man. An otter was gay man who was somewhere in between.

We classified ourselves into different tribes including clean-cut, daddy, discreet, geek, jock, leather, poz, rugged, or trans. Some of these terms were self-explanatory. Someone who identified as discreet was not out in public while someone who identified as poz was HIV positive. We also identified ourselves as tops or bottoms. These position-based descriptors signalled whether we took the insertive or penetrative role in anal sex. Those who specified versatile had no preference.

Beyond this basic vocabulary, I came across racialised terms such as rice queen, sticky rice, and panda bear. A rice queen was a non-Asian man who was exclusively attracted to Asian men to the point of fetishisation. The term sticky rice described Asian men who were exclusively sexually attracted to other Asian men. Lastly, a panda bear was an Asian version of a bear.

As people could simply mask their discrimination as sexual and romantic preference, rejection was more explicit on these social media platforms. Some people openly stated their "No fats, femmes, or Asians" policy on their profiles. At least this meant

I could easily avoid people who used outwardly fatphobic, misogynistic, and racist language. Some people felt no shame fetishising my racialised body. No matter who someone was in the real world, everyone complied with the hierarchies determined by Pākehā white ideals of attractiveness. They did not design these virtual spaces to appease people from my demographic background.

Yet again, I received another message from a blank profile. I was in the process of blocking the blank profile, when a series of photos came through of an Asian man in his mid-twenties. Up until that point, I thought Queer Asian people did not exist.

"Can we meet up?" said the message.

"I'm Marco," I continued to read the barrage of messages. "I'm an international student from the Philippines. I'm lonely."

"Okay," I typed my reply. I had nothing better to do that evening and I was curious to meet another Queer Asian person. "Let's meet at the car park of the Countdown in Church Corner."

Within ten minutes, I was waiting in the car park. This was a neutral location. I was not so naive I would give away my personal details without meeting him first. I finally saw him crossing the road around midnight.

"Hi, you must be Marco," I extended out my hand to shake the stranger's hand.

Marco looked quite different from his photos. He was much older and a lot shorter than the photos suggested. We exchanged pleasantries in the car park. When I made the assessment that he was not a threat, I guided him to my flat.

"Would you like a drink?" I asked Marco when we arrived at my room. I could tell he was nervous. Maybe a drink would break the tension.

"Sure," Marco replied. He took a sip of the whisky and made a sour expression.

Maybe not.

"I'm studying for a master's in political science," Marco told me in hushed tones. "I was working in the non-profit sector in the Philippines, but I had to leave. I didn't have a choice."

Marco had had a successful life in the Philippines, but he was in the closet. Aotearoa was his opportunity to explore his sexuality.

"It's too bad I can't be myself in Christchurch either. Most of my Filipino friends are part of the church." Marco finished his story and took another strained sip of whisky.

There were many similarities between our experiences – both of us left home to navigate our sexuality – except it was much safer for me to be Queer in Aotearoa than it was to be a Queer person in the Philippines.

I took Marco's glass and placed it on the windowsill. I placed my hand on his shoulder and turned to give him a kiss. His lips were tense. We spent the night together and he left before daybreak. We met twice more before he left Ōtautahi, once for a coffee, and once on campus.

I still follow Marco's updates on Instagram. He is an incredible photographer; I can see that he is still trying to find that safe haven from his posts. Queer Asian men, like me, experience the same if not greater levels of hostility in virtual spaces than physical spaces. There was no love for me in Ōtautahi. Perhaps I was not meant for this path.

Content warning

This chapter contains references to body hatred and fatphobia; homophobia; mental illness and ableism; nudity; racism and racial slurs; substance use and abuse; and sexism.

The chapter starts overleaf.

6
to return to one's roots

Mumbai, Winter 2023

"I'm getting married in India," Akhil broke the news to me in the spring of 2022. "I want to invite both you and your partner to our wedding."

Shit. We were double-booked. Jake's friend was getting married that same week. "Congratulations!" I told Akhil. "Jake can't go. He's got a gay wedding to attend, but I'll be there to celebrate your big day. I did promise you, remember."

After twenty-eight hours and four airports, I was finally in Mumbai.

"Welcome to Mumbai!" Akhil greeted me as he picked me up from the airport. "Fuck, it's been ages, bro. Let's get a beer. I want you to meet my parents."

"We've got the *haldi* and *mehendi* tomorrow. I'll lend you a *kurta* for the ceremonies and the wedding. I still need to pick up some whisky for the after-party." Akhil ran through the week's itinerary like a business briefing as he wove through the traffic seamlessly.

After a hasty lunch, and a brief meeting with his parents, Akhil dropped me off at my hotel in the affluent suburbs of Hiranandani Gardens.

"One more beer before bed?" Akhil asked me.

We picked up some beers and and a few cigarettes from a roadside stall. Finally, a moment of peace as we savoured a cigarette on the suburban streets of Mumbai.

"It's going to be a busy week. The driver will pick you up in the morning. I can't wait for this to be over and done with."

The *haldi* occurred without incident the next day – although one of Akhil's numerous cousins, Kanta, was too enthusiastic during the ceremony and got turmeric paste in Akhil's eye.

As day became night, what was just an altar honouring Ganesha flawlessly transformed into a dance floor. The entrance was set up as a temporary bar, and Akhil's relatives sat around waiting for the after-party to begin.

I ordered a whisky and Thums Up and quickly sculled it back. I could not help noticing Kanta on the dance floor.

"Are you family?" I asked Kanta as I danced alongside him. This was a discreet way for me to ask if he was Queer.

"How did you know?" Kanta laughed and clapped his hands together. He made his way to the fire exit and gestured me towards him. "Let's go for a smoke."

I followed him out to the balcony and the familiar hot humid air, thick like soup, enveloped me with a full-bodied embrace.

"Now tell me, Sidney, how could you tell I was gay?" Kanta asked me, as he took a drag from his cigarette; he put one hand on the railing to balance himself.

"Between your taste in fashion, the dancing, and your attitude, it wasn't much of a guess to be honest," I joked. The whiskies and Thums Up were working its magic on me.

Earlier that afternoon, Kanta had worn a mustard kurta with a floral *saari* draped over his shoulder.

He was now wearing a smart suit jacket with slacks.

"My parents know I'm gay," Kanta confessed to me. "Some family know, while others don't. I don't care, as long as my parents don't mind."

Kanta and I stood there on the balcony savouring the momentary peace and quiet while we inhaled the nicotine into our lungs. Kanta watched me intently as I admired the Mumbai skyline from the balcony.

"Where the hell were you?" Akhil asked me when I went back inside. "You and Kanta were gone for hours! We thought you'd got lost."

"You know you two are the talk of the family right now," Akhil laughed and patted me on the back. He ruffled my hair as if I was his child. "What happens in Mumbai stays in Mumbai, but don't do anything you'll regret."

The next day, I dragged myself out of bed to meet the driver downstairs. I made my way to Juhu. The Mumbai traffic seemed extra intolerable as I tried to hold down my stomach. I remembered why I did not drink alcoholic mixers.

"How are you? I can't remember anything from last night," Kanta sent me a message on WhatsApp. "We should get lunch. I want to talk to you."

I checked in to the next hotel, and we made plans to meet at a trendy restaurant in Juhu. Akhil was meant to join me that afternoon, but he was running late – as usual.

"I have a boyfriend," Kanta told me while I picked at the pear and avocado salad in front of me. I had tried to order a Caesar salad, but Kanta was offended by my basic selection, and he had instructed me to order something else.

"He's my first real relationship," Kanta continued. "We're still trying to figure out what it means to be in a relationship."

"Your relationship can be whatever you want it to be," I tried to contribute to the conversation.

"I know that," Kanta responded matter-of-factly.

I briefly forgot that I was in Mumbai and not in Ōtautahi. It did not take me long to realise that the Queer experience was not universal.

"What's it like to be gay in New Zealand?" Kanta asked curiously.

I diverted my attention from the salad to the cheese fondue. I tried my best not to lose the crouton that was hanging precariously from my fork.

"It's not bad, but it sucks if you're not white." I reported it as it was. There was no point sugar-coating my experience. "There's a lot of racism in the community."

"Is that so?" Kanta considered my words. He then began to laugh. "Why would I leave Mumbai then? I have everything I need here. If you have enough money and come from the right caste, nobody cares if you're gay."

We finished our meal, and he dropped me off at the hotel. Ashish was waiting for me outside with an autorickshaw (tuk-tuk) ready to take me to the next engagement.

"There's a gay party later tonight if you're interested," Kanta told me as we parted ways. "I'd love to see you there."

On the day of Akhil's wedding, I saw Kanta again with his nephew. His nephew was barely two years old and was sound asleep with his head resting on his shoulder.

"Why would he leave?" I thought to myself. Kanta had access to his family, his language, and his culture. This was his home.

I felt estranged from my family. My language and culture were my only connection to home. Where was home and what does home look like for me?

Unlikely match
Hong Kong, Summer 2015

"I'm going to Hong Kong," I told Iain as we laid in bed. "Do you want to come with me?" "Of course, it'll be fun!" Iain replied enthusiastically.

It was the summer of 2015. I had invited Iain to come with me to Hong Kong after dating him for only a few weeks. Even though our relationship only lasted the summer, the tickets were already booked and there was nothing I could do about it. Thankfully, we were still good friends.

Mum wanted my brother and me to go to Hong Kong so we could collect our Hong Kong identity cards. My brother went the year previously, and it was now my turn to go back. Our Mum secretly wanted us to move back to Hong Kong for work or study so she would have an excuse to be with her family and friends.

「咩話.」 (What?) Mum did not sound pleased.

「我個朋友想同我一齊去香港.」 (My friend wants to visit Hong Kong with me.) I told her as I booked our flight tickets.

My parents were very private people and did not like or appreciate the intrusion of strangers. This was why we never had sleepovers as children.

I met Mum in Sydney, and we travelled onwards to Hong Kong as a pair. It was after 清明 festival, which signalled the start of the typhoon season. I smelt the electricity in the air and the humidity clung to my skin.

Mum and I were staying in different locations – I was staying with an auntie in Tseung Kwan O (將軍澳) while Mum was staying with other family in Quarry Bay (魚涌). This incidental arrangement ensured maximum privacy.

The first thing I did when I landed in Hong Kong was open Grindr and Tinder. I did not know what to expect as I had only ever used these platforms in Ōtautahi where I was often greeted with "no fats, no femmes, no Asians", but instead I received notification after notification.

The last time I had been in Hong Kong was for a brief layover in 2012. I was finally around people who looked and sounded like me for the first time. The number of people on those platforms also impressed me. I did not expect there to be a thriving Queer community. Frankly, I did not expect to see other Queer and Cantonese people like me. It was the first time I was aware that there were people who shared my language, my culture, my world view, and my sexuality. I felt liberated. Even though I was under constant surveillance around my family, I was in a city of seven million people. There was little risk I would encounter anyone that could out me to my family. I could broaden the confines of my closet. I still muted my notifications as a precaution.

There was one person I did know in Hong Kong – Martin, who I had met in Germany. He was studying in Canada, but he was home for the summer. I wanted to meet up with him so I could ask him questions on what it was like to grow up in Hong Kong. As fate would have it, I was lying in bed swiping through Tinder, when I saw a familiar profile picture. He used the same profile picture for Facebook. This was the night before we were meant to meet up. I did not expect to see his profile and I suddenly felt like an intruder.

「你好嗎，好耐冇見.」(How are you? I have not seen you in a long time.) I yelled across the crowd to Martin. He was waiting for me on the other side of the subway station.

Martin heard my voice and made his way towards me. He wove through the impenetrable crowds and ended up on my side of the station.

I reached out to Martin for a hug. He reciprocated my hug, but I could sense the awkward energy between us. It was probably because we barely knew each other, or perhaps he knew that I saw him on Tinder. It did not matter then.

「真係好耐冇見，你點呀.」 (It really has been a while. How have you been?) Martin greeted me courteously.

Martin guided me through the narrow streets of Tsim Sha Tsui and we arrived at the English-style restaurant he wanted to take me to.

「返學返成點呀.」 (How was school?) I asked Martin with genuine curiosity.

「係咁啦.」 (It's okay.) Martin responded as he flicked through the menu.

As Martin and I warmed up to each other, we became more talkative. Over the course of the meal, we talked about how our lives had changed since we last saw each other. We reminisced about our time in Germany, and we compared our experiences of living in Canada and Aotearoa.

The whole time Martin and I talked, I held on to his secret. I waited for the right time to mention what I saw the night before.

"I saw you on Tinder," I confessed to Martin when it was finally time for us to leave. "Also, I think I'm gay."

I did not know what else to say. I did not want to out Martin in public. At this point we switched to English. Maybe this would offer us a bit more privacy.

"I know," Martin whispered quietly. "I also saw you. I didn't know what to say." "Then why did you not swipe right on me!" I joked.

Martin laughed. Maybe a joke is what we needed to break the tension. I could sense in that moment that we went from acquaintances to friends.

"I've still got time," Martin told me as we settled the bill. "Should we go for a walk?"

We walked along the busy streets of Tsim Sha Tsui, and people surrounded us. The perfect place for a heart-to-heart conversation.

"I came out to myself last year," Martin told me. "I told Mum about my feelings recently, but she told me not to mention anything to Dad."

"Same here," I replied and recounted my experiences so far.

Martin and I continued to talk as we ventured through the winding streets of Tsim Sha Tsui. The further we walked, the more we talked about our struggles. He was the first person I could openly talk to about my identity in English and Cantonese. We both felt in and out of the closet.

Diverging worlds
Hong Kong, Summer 2015

As my time in Hong Kong progressed, I became more empowered. I messaged anyone who was interested in me. I felt bolder knowing that I was not in the minority.

I wanted to meet other Queer people who could help me verbalise the feelings I had internalised. I knew some students from Ōtautahi, so I used them as an excuse to venture out. Thankfully, this did not raise any suspicions with Mum.

Iain arrived a week after me and he stayed with me at my aunt's apartment. We shared my cousin's bunk bed who was boarding with my parents in Aotearoa. I was in the top bunk, and I fantasised about what we would have been doing had we still been together.

「你知道 係基架呵.」 (You know he's gay, right?) My auntie warned me one evening while Iain was in the bathroom.

「有咩問題呢.」 (What's the problem?) I told my auntie, quite rightfully. Iain was not discreet about his Queerness, but it did not matter.

「你唔係基嘩.」 (Well, you're not gay, right?) My auntie joked. I thought she was expecting a definitive answer from me.

「基唔基有點呢.」 (Does it matter if I'm gay or not?) I asked my auntie in return.

My aunt and I cut short our exchange when Iain returned to the lounge. It was quite clear that there was still a lot of work to do before I could come out to my family. I first had to learn the language to help me put these feelings into words. One person who helped me to externalise my feelings was Nathaniel who I met on Tinder.

"I have a boyfriend," Nathaniel told me. "Why would he care if I'm here to meet people?"

I was curious with his arrangement. I met him in Kowloon, and he took me to a Korean barbecue restaurant. I was surprised by how comfortable he was talking about his Queer identity.

"I realised I was gay when I was in the US," Nathaniel said while grilling beef. "I came out to Mum, but she told me not to tell Dad."

"Are you going to come out to your dad?" I asked curiously.

Nathaniel's story sounded remarkably similar.

"What's the point? Why would I want to ruin the balance of my family for a romantic relationship?" he replied, frankly. It was not worth the hassle.

After dinner, we took the MTR to Tsing Yi (青衣). We walked past a bamboo theatre erected in honour of Tin Hau 天后. Many worshippers across the Southern Chinese coast still know her as 媽祖 (Ancestral Mother).

We know Tin Hau as the protector of seafarers. One version of the myth spoke of how she saved her family who were caught out at sea during a typhoon. Tin Hau risked her life, fell into a trance, and chanted to the heavens asking for the safe return of her family. Her father and brother returned to shore unscathed, and she was deified for her miracle. Her dedication to her family is the reason there are still hundreds, if not thousands, of temples built in her honour. Tin Hau was the exemplary child willing to sacrifice her life for her family.

"We can't all be like her," Nathaniel joked as we walked past the altar. We stood in front of the Ancestral Mother and bowed three times before moving on.

「值唔值得含洋腸.」 (Is the Western dick worth it?) Nathaniel asked me as he listened to me recount my experience in Aotearoa.

"Do you know why you're always expected to be a bottom?" Nathaniel continued with his lecture. "It's because white people think they're still colonisers. They colonised our land. They colonised our people. And now they want to colonise your hole."

"Why don't you find yourself a Cantonese boy who looks like you and understands your culture? You can't be colonised again by your own people."

"But what about the Chinese in Mainland China." I asked Nathaniel. I had never had someone speak to me with such honesty.

"What about them?" Nathaniel laughed. "You don't think the Northerners wouldn't colonise us if they had the chance?"

"It doesn't matter if you're gay or straight. When the communists took over the Mainland in 1949, we were no longer one people. You can go back to your ancestral village, but that no longer exists. We will never be the same."

"Sidney, don't be so naive. Don't take things for granted. How many times do you need to be colonised before you realise how fucked up the world actually is? We need to create our own futures. That is the only way we can find balance."

Next station
Hong Kong, Summer 2015

I mulled over Nathaniel's words, but I wanted to sample Hong Kong one more time. I went back on Grindr one last time. The stranger from Grindr told me to meet him outside de Spa Chocolatier. I snuck away from my friends who were still clubbing in Lan Kwai Fong 蘭桂坊.

"I'll send my location," the stranger instructed me.

When I received the location, I made my way towards the rendezvous point. The streets were dark and quiet. The sleepless city was asleep for once.

"You must be Sidney." I heard a voice from the shadows.

The stranger emerged from the darkness.

"I'm dying for a drink. I saw a 7-Eleven around the corner," The stranger suggested. "I'm Lucas by the way. I've just flown in from London."

I followed Lucas to the 7-Eleven. The storefront was lit like a beacon on the hollow street. "I'm Sidney." I tried to make conversation. "I was just in Lan Kwai Fong with my friends from New Zealand."

"I do recognise that accent!" Lucas commented. "I've spent time in Auckland."

Lucas took a six-pack of Asahi from the fridge. He stopped me from paying at the counter while he fumbled around with his wallet. He took out his newly minted Octopus card.

"Come with me," Lucas instructed me. "I'll take you upstairs."

Lucas pointed towards a dimly lit building, and I followed his directions. As we entered the building, the security guard inspected me intently from his desk as I entered the elevator with my new companion.

"My work has put me up here while I find a place of my own. I've just started my new job as a journalist in the city," Lucas told me. "I hope you don't mind it."

I walked out on to the balcony and observed the city below. The waves on Victoria Harbour reflected the light off the skyscrapers and the boats. I could see why people called Hong Kong the "Pearl of the Orient".

Lucas held me close to him and gently kissed me on the neck. We spent the night in a deep embrace while the city woke up beneath us.

「下一站寶琳」 (Next station Po Lam)

"Did you meet anyone last night?" Iain asked me when we met up the next morning.

We met outside the subway station so my auntie would not suspect that Iain and I had not been together the whole night.

"I did," I replied coyly. "How about you? Did you meet anyone?" "I did indeed," Iain gleamed.

「下一站羅湖」 (Next station Lo Wu)

"Are you back in Hong Kong yet?" Lucas asked me excitedly on WhatsApp a few days later. I was in Mainland China for three days. I felt like I was there much longer.

"Yes, I'm back!" I messaged back quickly.

"Can we meet up?" he replied instantaneously. "We need to celebrate!"

When we cleared customs, I said goodbye to Mum, and I took the train to meet Lucas.

「下一站香港大學」 (Next station HKU)

I wandered around the train station aimlessly. Lucas had instructed me to meet him outside.

"It was a mission to get this, but I'm glad it's finally arrived," Lucas told me.

Lucas proudly flashed his new Hong Kong identification card in front of my face. "There's also something else I want to show you. Follow me!"

I followed him down the busy streets of Sai Wan 西灣. It was late afternoon, and the street hawkers were busy setting up their stalls. We turned into a cul-de-sac.

"I just got the keys to my new apartment," Lucas told me as he fumbled with his keys.

Lucas gave the door a firm push and we were greeted with a modest sized apartment.

"How do you like it?" Lucas asked me for my approval.

"It's nice," I told him as I ran my fingers along the fresh bed sheets. Lucas grabbed my arm and pulled me into him. He kissed me on the lips.

"Welcome home," Lucas told me and kissed me on the lips.

「下一站西營盤」 (Next station Sai Ying Pun)

The last time I met Lucas was also my last night in Hong Kong. I told Mum I would be out partying with friends. One more lie. I wanted to spend my last night with Lucas.

We walked down Third Street 第三街. The pavement was wet and reflected the neon-lit signs. As we walked together, we quietly acknowledged the life around us. The lights shone through the barred windows on to the steep road, and we listened to the dull humming of ancient air-conditioning units.

"You didn't have to do that," I scolded Lucas jokingly. We had just had dinner and he had made a big deal about paying for our meal. "Why didn't you let me pay for dinner?"

"When I was nineteen, I went on a date with an older man." Lucas began telling me his story. "He was only ten years older than me. And like you, I tried to pay for dinner."

"He told me I didn't need to pay, because one day I'd find myself in a similar situation." Lucas continued narrating his story as we walked down the street side by side. "One day I'll be on a date with a younger man, and it'll be my turn to pay."

"After that date, I never saw him again." Lucas's voice lingered with a hint of melancholy. "I guess today was the day."

As I reflected on Lucas's story, I wondered if the path I had chosen was a lonely path. Was I destined to be alone for the rest of my life? Was I destined, like Lucas, and those that came before him, to sojourn from one relationship to another – never to find a sense of balance?

We went upstairs to Lucas's apartment. He undressed me and he held me close to his chest. We stood there in a trance, slowly swaying to the music. *Yellow Flicker Beat* played in the background. It was our last night together. He led me to his bed. He kissed my neck. He then kissed my navel. I listened to the sound of traffic in the background. The moist air hung heavy on my skin. I held on to Lucas one last time.

「下一站北角」 (Next station North Point)

The next morning, I was the only person on the train. What was meant to be a simple holiday became a monumental turning point in my life. I realised that staying in the closet was not my only option, but what other alternatives were there for people like me?

My journey had ended. It was time for me to go home.

「請勿靠近車門」 (Please mind the gap)

Content warning

This chapter contains references to abuse; homophobia; hospitalisation; mental illness and ableism; nudity; racism and racial slurs; self-harm and suicidal thoughts, intentions, and actions; substance use and abuse; swear words or curse words; and violence.

The chapter starts overleaf.

7
to find comfort in a hopeless situation

Ōtautahi, Winter 2015

When I came back to Aotearoa, I was desperate to have the same conversations I had had with Martin and Nathaniel. I was desperate to experience the same feelings I had had with Lucas. But I was no longer in Hong Kong.

It was during this time that Christchurch Pride was building momentum in the community. I went to one of their events at Mashina, which was a basement bar under the local casino.

There were hundreds of people on the dance floor. They were all watching the drag artists lip-syncing to Nineties pop songs. I was there alone, and I stood next to the water dispenser. I wanted to be discreet and far away from the crowd.

"What's a handsome thing like you doing back here?" A stranger approached me at the back of the venue. He was wearing a leather harness. Glitter and sequins coated his dense chest and shoulder hair.

"I'm good," I replied to the stranger. "I just feel out of place. I don't think I belong here."

"Well," the stranger replied as he poured himself a glass of water. "You're only going to have as much fun as you let yourself."

"Perhaps I'll see you next time?" the stranger told me as he gave me a parting hug. He walked away and disappeared into the crowd.

I went home shortly after this interaction with the stranger. Despite not having lived in Hong Kong, I felt a greater sense of belonging with the Queer people I had met there. I felt like an intruder when I was in Ōtautahi. This did not feel like home.

I was once again greeted with lukewarm responses on both Tinder and Grindr. I had no love for Ōtautahi, and there was no love for me. The only times I had any success was when I was outside of Ōtautahi – in Tāmaki Makaurau or Te Whanganui-a-Tara.

Paul was one lasting connection I made on Tinder while I was in Tāmaki Makaurau. It was after my road trip with Jochim, Lotte, and Menno in the motor home. We matched before I left Tāmaki Makaurau and we continued messaging throughout the trip.

When I returned to Tāmaki Makaurau, Paul took me out to dinner and then introduced me to the strange and wonderful world of Family Bar on Karangahape Road. For the uninitiated, Family is a multi-storey gay bar with two dance floors and three separate bars.

Family was hosting a drag competition that night. The room was filled with smoke and drunken revellers. Paul and I were dancing in harmony to the strobe lights. He pushed me against the wall, and we kissed in full view of the public.

We returned to Paul's apartment in Newmarket overlooking the train station, and we spent the night together. The next day he dropped me off at the bus stop on Queens Street, where I took the overnight bus back to Te Whanganui-a-Tara.

When I came back to Aotearoa, I reconnected with Paul in Tāmaki Makaurau in search of those much sought after conversations and experiences I needed. The second time I met with Paul, we did not have the same spark.

My trip to Hong Kong had left me with a sense of emptiness. My need to fill this emptiness propelled me into the next period of my journey. This included a number of unnecessary risks leaving me with lasting consequences that I still carry with me today.

Crisis of faith
Te Whanganui-a-Tara, Autumn 2015

I matched with Jono while I was in Te Whanganui-a-Tara. He was my first relationship since Iain. We started talking before he asked me to add him on Facebook to talk there instead.

"Add me on my alt account," Jono told me one day. "My family are Māori and very Christian. Only my closest friends know I'm gay."

"They sent me to a guidance counsellor to fix me and convinced me I should be a pastor," Jono continued with his story. "I really thought I was broken before I ran away. Here I am in Wellington, working as a hotel manager."

After a few weeks of talking to each other, I booked my flights to see Jono in Te Whanganui-a-Tara. This time I went home without my parents' knowledge. This trip to Te Whanganui-a-Tara was for me.

Jono met me at the airport. I expected a kiss, but he shook my hand briskly. I attempted a hug, but he was visibly uncomfortable. The only time he expressed any affection was when he gently touched my hand at the back of the bus.

"We're going to stay in my room in the hotel," Jono told me as he led me up a staircase. "Don't mention to anyone we're together though."

The room was overlooking Courtney Place. As Jono shut the door to his room, he turned around and kissed me on the lips. He pushed me against the wall.

"You have no idea how long I've been waiting for this moment," Jono told me as he began to undress me.

"I've got a surprise for you," Jono told me as we walked down the waterfront. It was late afternoon, and the sea was calm. It reflected the orange gold hues of the sunset. "I remember you telling me that you've always wanted to go to Shed 5."

I had an incredible weekend with Jono. When I got back to Ōtautahi, I was already planning my next trip to see Jono.

A month before Jono was meant to visit me in Ōtautahi, I sensed something was off. Jono was drinking every day and his behaviour was getting more erratic.

"I met someone on Tinder," Jono confessed to me one afternoon. "It was only for a drink. I'm just on there to meet people."

Since I was no longer tied to my phone, I began investing my time at the gym working on my fitness. Brandon, a colleague from the insurance company, was happy to show me how to work out at the gym.

"I know that you're cheating on me," Jono spluttered over the phone. He was drunk. "I know you're not at the gym."

"What are you talking about? Are you okay?" I asked in confusion. I had just got out of Brandon's car, and I saw a few missed calls from Jono. "I've been at the gym all this time, why don't you believe me?"

"Don't fucking lie to me, I know you're fucking cheating on me," Jono continued in a frenzy. "You know what; I'm just going to fucking end it. I've got some pills under my bed."

Jono hung up on me and I was at a loss for what to do. I tried to call his friends, but no one picked up. I had no choice but to call the police.

"Fire, ambulance, or police. What's your emergency?" the operator asked me.

"My long-distance boyfriend wants to kill himself. I'm in another city and I can't get hold of his friends," I told the operator frantically.

"We'll see what we can do," the operator told me calmly and transferred me to another line.

I waited patiently with my flatmates around me as I explained the situation to the police. I gave them the key code to the building and guided the police to his room. They managed to get hold of him, and shortly after, I received a message from his friend.

"Jono's been admitted to the psychiatric unit," Jono's friend told me. "What you did was really shitty; you should've been here for him."

Our last exchange was over email. Jono asked me to pay him back for the return flights to Ōtautahi. I paid him back without hesitation. I blocked him and never spoke to him again.

Chill out time
Ōtautahi, Winter 2015

My relationship with Jono left me broken. I was scared of people, and I felt more alone and disconnected from the wider Queer community. I decided to take a break from exploring physical and virtual spaces. I turned my focus to study so I could finish my degree and leave Ōtautahi for the last time. I had a few connections left from the university. One of these connections was Mitchell who I had met at a university club. Mitchell was a geology student, and we had the pleasure of being part of a university club, which was in essence more like a cult, together.

"Hey man, how's it going?" Mitchell greeted me from the driver's seat. He gestured his head towards the back seat. "This is Ashish by the way. He's an international student from India."

Ashish was sitting, chilling, in the back seat. Mitchell was busy talking to Brian who was in the passenger seat.

"Yo, what's up man?" Ashish greeted me.

"Hey, how's it going?" I wanted to make the effort to sound enthusiastic. "I know I just met you, but I'm going through a really shit time. I just broke up with my boyfriend. Sorry, ex-boyfriend. I'm a bit gutted at the moment."

"That sucks man," Ashish responded with the right level of sympathy.

"Yeah, it does suck. Can you keep a secret? Mitchell doesn't know I'm gay," I told him in hushed tones.

"Want to get drunk?" Ashish suggested with genuine interest.

"Fuck it, why not?" I replied far too enthusiastically.

Ashish and I were an unlikely pair. Since he just lived down the street from me, we would often meet and drink until the early hours of the morning. We often joked that we were the Ōtautahi version of *Harold and Kumar*. My favourite memory with Ashish was probably our road trip around Te Waipounamu over the Easter weekend with a colleague from the insurance company. I cannot for the life of me remember what we were arguing about, but we spent the whole weekend arguing, drinking beer, sightseeing, arguing, settling on our differences of opinion, and arguing some more. Astonishingly, Ashish and I are still very good friends today, one who I might even call my best friend if he would give me the honour.

It was through Ashish that I met Akhil, Amit, and Neil. I brought them with me to house parties, and more often than not, we were regularly the only non-whites in these spaces. It brought me a lot of joy to disrupt these white spaces, and the hosts would normally be happy with this injection of diversity. During this interlude of my coming out journey, I probably drank too, smoked too much, and ate too much. But it also gave me time and space to reconnect with other aspects of my identity I had neglected in this white closet.

I spent a lot of time during this period thinking about how my Cantonese-identity interplayed with my Aotearoa-born identity. My childhood trauma from racism had marred my perceptions of what it meant to be a "Kiwi" or a "New Zealander". I still remember being scolded by a *whaea* (aunty) at a *marae* (meeting ground) after a misguided white teacher told me to call myself as Pākehā in my *pepeha* (formal greeting) in primary school. How was I to know my identity was being assimilated into whiteness? This *whakamā* (shame) had made me hide my identity, until I met a group of people who did not care who I was meant to be. They were some of the first people with a migrant background around my age who I could speak to openly and frankly. Their perspectives on their identity, often mediated through beer and a hookah pipe, helped me coalesce these two disparate aspects of my identity.

When people asked them, "Where are you from?", they would very happily answer "India" without hesitation. For them, being an outsider was a given. The same question would elicit a quite different response from people, like me, who had been born and grew up in Aotearoa. We were brought up with an unrealistic expectation to assimilate into whiteness. This is because we were socialised into whiteness through the process of racialisation. This is why when people ask me where I am from, it is not only a constant reminder that I do not belong, but also a reminder that I will never be white.

Over the course of nearly a decade, my friendships with Ashish, Akhil, Amit, and Neil have ebbed and flowed, but they are probably the closest group of people I would describe as my best friends. This is especially true for Ashish who has no trouble challenging me on my privilege and entitlement. I had to relearn how to perceive the world without the white lens. Even though I remained largely in the closet throughout this period, at least

I had the time to nurture my Cantonese-*tauiwi* (non-Māori) identity in a friendly and safe space.

Tipping point
Ōtautahi, Spring 2015

On the outside, I had Ashish, Akhil, Amit, and Neil to support me socially, but mentally and emotionally, I was on a downward spiral with my coming out journey. I no longer cared about the types of interactions I had with men in Ōtautahi. I was obsessed with the idea of becoming an object of desire. I was no longer interested in finding a community. Despite my negative past experiences, I once again returned to Cruz to meet men for sex. I returned home one evening with a tourist from Brazil. We were both drunk and he offered to drive me home. In hindsight, this was an idiotic decision as I could have very well have got myself killed.

With my lowered inhibitions, I leant into my impulses and increased the number of risky sexual interactions. I was at a party in Upper Riccarton when I received a message from Daniel and Craig on Grindr. They were bored and felt like experimenting, so I went to their house without assessing the danger.

When I arrived at the house, Daniel offered me a whisky and soda. Craig then whisked me away to Daniel's room where I laid down on the bed. They tied my wrists to the headboard. Daniel went to get a box from the cupboard while Craig undressed me.

"Have you done anything like this before?" Daniel asked me as he opened the box and took out more rope.

"I'll try anything at least once," I replied.

"Perfect," Craig said as he lightly bit my nipple.

Everything had a price, and the price I paid for my risky sexual behaviour was my mental and physical health. Within weeks of my spree, I started to experience symptoms and I was beginning to worry. I thought I could ignore the symptoms, but the symptoms reared their ugly head when it stopped me from establishing a genuine connection.

Before I began experiencing the symptoms, I met Cyril on Tinder. He worked as a bartender for Calendar Girls – the local strip club.

"Can we please go on a date?" Cyril asked me one evening after messaging for weeks.

"Of course," I agreed reluctantly. Cyril was lovely and I did not have the heart to reject him. Cyril took me out for dinner at Mexicanos, but I could not enjoy his company as the whole time I felt uncomfortable because of the symptoms. When we finished dinner, he asked me if I wanted to go for a walk.

"Do you want to see what's upstairs?" Cyril asked me with a childish grin as we walked past Calendar Girls.

"Sure, why not?" I agreed and followed Cyril to a room upstairs. At the centre of the room was a round bed surrounded by red velvet wallpaper. "Where do you even get a round bed?"

Cyril held me against him, and we kissed to the vibrations of the bass from downstairs. Cyril put his hand on my belt, and I pushed him away.

"I should go now," I told him. I gave him one last kiss, before I went home.

I was ashamed of myself. I felt disgusted with the symptoms. I felt disgusted with my decisions that led me to this point. The next day I made an appointment with the sexual health clinic as I knew the symptoms would not go away without help.

"Have you considered Gardasil?" the nurse asked me.

"What is that?" I responded in confusion.

"It reduces your chances of catching STIs like this in the future," she explained. "It's currently not funded for men, so it'll set you back $90 a dose. You will need three doses. We will not charge you to administer the vaccine, but you will need to bring us the dose yourself. We don't stock the vaccine at the clinic. Make sure to get it to us within two hours before it expires."

"Anyway, I'll give you some paste for your current symptoms," she continued "And I'll check in on you in a few weeks to see if it's cleared."

"How about a routine sexual health check-up then? Just in case," she added.

The next few weeks were both a physical and emotional test. I travelled down to Ōtepoti with my parents to attend my brother's graduation. I frequently excused myself to go to the bathroom to apply more paste. I was restless. I could not sit still at the ceremony. I was in agony.

"What would my family think if they found out?" I thought to myself.

Eventually the symptoms cleared. I still think about that period until this day.

A year later, I received a message from Cyril.

"I hope you're doing well. I really liked you. It was a shame we didn't work out," Cyril told me. "I'm in Sydney now. I'm going to study history."

"Same here," I thought to myself.

As of 1 January 2017, Gardasil is now fully funded by the Aotearoa government for everyone aged 9 to 26. The vaccine reduces the risk of HPV-related cancer.

My risky behaviour was not sustainable. I realised I needed the support of a community.

Content warning

This chapter contains references to homophobia; racism and racial slurs; and transphobia.

The chapter starts overleaf.

8

to sail against the tide

Ōtautahi, Summer 2018

With the trauma of Jono and my health struggles now behind me, I began obsessively consuming Queer programming like *Please Like Me* (2013), *EastSiders* (2012), and *RuPaul's Drag Race* (2009). I watched these shows repeatedly, with multiple viewings for each episode, trying to find a deeper meaning behind what it meant to be Queer beyond sexual desires. I found it difficult to relate to these stories. Most of these stories were based in the US or narrated from a white perspective. I wanted to relate to a common experience.

I turned to social media to find a semblance of a community. Perhaps I could expand my perspectives through the lived experiences of other recognisably Queer people in Aotearoa. Unfortunately, most of the visibly Queer people I found on social media were in Tāmaki Makaurau and Te Whanganui-a-Tara. I felt even more alone in Ōtautahi. It is true that 「遠水不能救近火」 (water from afar cannot put out a nearby fire), I needed to find support from my immediate surroundings. Even though it felt like a wasted exercise at the time, I am still grateful for the people I met through social media like the collection editor – Kia ora, Patrick!

I looked up a Queer support group based in Ōtautahi called Qtopia, which is a social support service for Queer young people, their whanau and communities. The purpose of the organisation was to create positive social change through education, advocacy, support, and celebration. Previously, I did not feel secure enough with my sexuality to attend, but now that I had come to terms with my identity, I realised that I had much more to gain by being connected. It was there that I first met Joy and Courtney – the managing director and second-in-command of the support service.

"Kia ora, my angels!" Joy would greet everyone warmly at each support group, before we took turns doing a round of names, pronouns, and personal updates.

It was at the social support group where I met Kyla, a Malaysian Chinese transwoman, who had migrated to Ōtautahi. She was the first Queer Asian person I spoke to in a public space. It felt surreal to have open and honest conversations about our experiences of being Queer and Asian in Ōtautahi. After another successful support group socialising with other young Queer people, Kyla and I left together and went home on the same bus.

"When did you realise you were different?" I asked Kyla.

"I've always felt different. I'm sure even you knew you felt different," Kyla commented. "You're right. I've never felt a sense of belonging as an Asian in New Zealand, but I've also never felt like I belonged in Queer spaces either," I continued.

"Me neither," Kyla replied. "It's taken me a long time to come out as trans, and I don't know if my family will ever understand me. But that's okay, at least now I can be me."

"Will I see you again?" I asked Kyla as our bus rolled to a stop.

"Maybe. Maybe next week." Kyla waved at me as she got off the bus.

After that night, I never saw or spoke to Kyla again. Kyla later added me on Facebook, and I still see her updates. She returned to Malaysia to be with her family, but she no longer presented as female. I hope she is happy, and she can still be herself. I learnt from our fleeting encounter that our experiences were not unique. Many Queer Asians felt the same sense of isolation.

Looking out
Ōtautahi, Autumn 2023

I was in a lab meeting with my supervisors, other researchers and PhD students working on natural language processing. I had been working on my PhD for over a year now. At my PhD confirmation, I proposed that I would model the social and linguistic characteristics of local populations using georeferenced digital language data. In short, I was attempting to find evidence that non-geographic dialects are emerging on social media.

I was content with this topic because I was interested in this area of computational linguistics. I also did not want to do my PhD research on anything identity related, as I was not willing to have my identity scrutinised through academic frameworks. However, as I progressed through my PhD, I realised that my area of research and my passion in supporting our Queer communities were diverging into two very separate paths. I was beginning to regret my initial decision to not incorporate any aspect of my Queer identity. I felt like a coward.

In the lab meeting, I put forward the idea that we should work on a shared task for an upcoming workshop on equality, diversity, and inclusion in computational linguistics. The objective of the shared task was to implement a classification model to detect homophobia and transphobia in social media comments in English, Spanish, Hindi, Tamil, and Malayalam. Even though I did not intend to contribute to Queer research through my PhD, at least I could use my skills to advance a small area in this space. I proposed that we train a classification model on the labelled homophobic and transphobic social media comments with pre-trained language models (PLMs).

"What are your thoughts? Do you think this is a good idea?" I asked my supervisor.

"I know how involved you are in the Queer community," my supervisor told me. "There's no harm in combining your research interests and what you're enthusiastic about."

"You know how easily I get distracted," I confessed to my supervisor.

"We can always find a way to include this into your main thesis," my supervisor suggested. This was a gamble as training language models are notoriously time-consuming and computationally expensive. At best, I would have learnt a new skill, but going on a research tangent like this would inevitably eat into my PhD. I thought long and hard, before it dawned on me how I could synthesise my research and my passion.

"If I do find evidence that digital dialects are emerging, then PLMs would be considerably biased based on the initial training data," I told my supervisor excitedly. "Then the accuracy of our classification model would also be biased if we don't fine-tune the PLMs for dialect variety."

"This means even if we trained a classification model in English to detect homophobia and transphobia for social media comments in the US, then the same model wouldn't work as well in New Zealand, India, or any other country where digital dialects are emerging. Homophobia and transphobia are going to be expressed differently depending on country, language, or register. Maybe we should fine-tune these PLMs by dialect!"

"Good thinking," my supervisor replied. "This will come together more as you work on it." We are still a long way away from knowing whether this method will work. But the purpose of this story is not about my PhD research, computational linguistics, or PLMs, it was the fact that I could bring in my Queer perspective into my work as an out Queer Asian, which is a luxury I wish that I had had early on in my research journey when I was still in the closet.

When I finally left my role at the insurance company, I returned to university to finish my degree. I once again found myself with limited choices. My first option was to go home. My parents saw this as the only option. Alternatively, option two – I had to find a reason to stay in Ōtautahi. I had close friends like Ashish, Akhil, and Amit and I started to form a community. I decided to stay in Ōtautahi. I figured I needed the time to continue with my journey to find a sense of balance with my identities. I automatically enrolled in the honours programme.

"Just one more year," I thought to myself.

The head of department convinced me to apply for the departmental scholarship and convert my honours to a master's in Linguistics. This gave me the opportunity to carry out original research. When they offered me a scholarship, I went to my supervisor to explore research topics within the field of Lavender Linguistics. This is the study of language used by Queer communities. They were the only openly Queer academic in the department.

I wanted to place myself within their research interests to position myself within Queer spaces. I wanted to be adjacent to Queerness, but I still was not ready to come out. I would learn about Queer identities while I kept my identity hidden. Maybe I could do this to navigate Queerness without coming out. I often wonder how being in the closet influenced my research trajectory. "Maybe I could analyse the speech features of gay men?" I asked my supervisor naively. "But what benefit will this bring to their community?" my supervisor posed these fundamental questions to me. "How can this piece of research be weaponised against their community?"

I sat there in their office, and I thought hard about the ethical implications of my research proposition. How could my research be weaponised to prosecute people like me? After much back and forth, we settled on a research topic. My supervisor tasked me to explore the vocal satisfaction of transmasculine individuals. This was an extension of their research on the communicative needs of transgender and non-conforming peoples.

Before I began this project, I had an extremely poor understanding of the needs of transgender and gender non-conforming peoples. I was deeply grateful that my supervisor trusted me to conduct this piece of research. This gave me an opportunity to develop my understanding of the needs within our Queer communities. I worked with my supervisor and other Queer academics to create an online survey. As part of the survey, I also collected speech samples of transmasculine individuals.

I felt a sense of comfort with my role as a researcher. I observed Queer spaces from my closet. My interactions were research interactions. Meanwhile, I used this as an opportunity to conduct my own environmental scan of what services and resources were available. I spent hours browsing through websites, blogs, and Facebook pages. I felt a sense of security knowing that I could justify my behaviour as an academic and not as an individual. I reached out to Queer organisations in Ōtautahi and across Aotearoa. Organisations like Qtopia, Christchurch Pride, Rainbow Youth, InsideOut, and more. I advertised my research online, but I felt an immense level discomfort with my behaviour.

"Is it okay for an outsider like me to message these groups?" I asked my supervisor repeatedly. "Are you sure you're not part of the community?" my supervisor asked me in return. "Not even a little non-binary?"

"No," I replied with complete certainty. These days I am not so sure.

Why would the Queer community trust a stranger like me? I could not even be honest with myself about my sexuality – why would anyone trust me to understand their needs?

"I'm consciously trying to change my voice."

"I feel self-conscious about how strangers perceive my voice."

"My voice frustrates me."

"I have a speaking voice that feels authentic to me."

"Your voice reflects the true you."

Many of the questions I posed in the survey could have been questions I should have been asking myself. My research became an introspective exercise. All I had to do was replace voice with identity.

"I'm consciously trying to change my identity."

"I feel self-conscious about how strangers perceive my identity."

"My identity frustrates me."

"I have an identity that feels authentic to me."

"Your identity reflects the true you."

I submitted my master's thesis on Tuesday, 20 November 2017. Coincidentally this was also the Transgender Remembrance Day. Was this another fateful coincidence? While I became more confident with my Queer identity in an academic setting, I could feel the metaphorical closet door closing. After spending a year being adjacent to Queerness, I was still not ready to come out.

When I finally submitted my thesis, I experienced both joy and immense sadness. My excuse to stay in Ōtautahi had run its course. My parents wanted me home. They expected me to fulfil my duties as their child. As I prepared myself to leave Ōtautahi, a government agency offered me an analyst role in Te Whanganui-a-Tara.

"Are you in a relationship?" the recruitment officer asked me.

"No, I'm not." I had no choice but to lie as I was seeing someone at the time.

However, the government agency had a stringent background screening process, and I was not willing to lie. How could I admit my sexuality to the government before I could admit my sexuality to my family, my friends, or myself? I felt like I had no choice but to turn it down. I declined the job offer, and I looked elsewhere. I could not go home just yet; I needed more time.

Just one more year.

Shortly afterwards, I began my role as a customer service officer at the Inland Revenue based in Ōtautahi. I needed time to continue exploring my identity. It was easy to hide who I was at the Inland Revenue. I processed GST returns in my role – a mundane job. I could easily mask my identity. I thought I would be safe if no one asked me about my personal life. I was not satisfied with my job. I did not study for almost five years in Linguistics to process GST returns. How many more excuses did I need to make before I could be my authentic self? I felt trapped.

Within six months, I applied for a data analyst job in the national statistics office. They tasked me to work alongside *hapū*, *iwi*, and Māori organisations to provide official statistics. It was an incredibly satisfying and meaningful role to support our Indigenous communities, but I felt I would not be able to be an effective ally if I continued to hide my identity. How could I build trust with Indigenous communities, who inherently distrust the government, if I did not even trust myself to be genuine or authentic? It was time for me to come out of the closet.

Just one more year.

Opening up
Te Awakairangi, Summer 2018

With a tentative deadline now in mind, it was time for me to unpack my closet. I began this process with Akhil who was my closest friend while he was in Te Awakairangi. Akhil wanted to see Te Whanganui-a-Tara, so I invited him to stay with me at home.

"I've got something to tell you," I announced from my bed. Akhil was on the mattress below. Akhil and I were staying in the spare bedroom. Mum was not too happy with this arrangement as I broke the cardinal rule of no sleepovers.

We were watching a pirated version of *Ae Dil Hai Mushkil* (2016) on my laptop. It was arguably a terrible movie, but we did not have much planned that night. We were halfway through the movie when I found the courage to come out to Akhil.

"What do you want to tell me?" Akhil responded to my surprise announcement. He got up from the mattress to pause the movie.

"I'm gay. I've been dating a guy. I was too worried to tell you because I didn't want it to come between our friendship," I confessed to Akhil. We were halfway through a bottle of honey whisky I had found in the pantry.

"Why would we stop being friends?" Akhil asked me. "If I did care that you were gay, I would've run out the door as soon as you told me. But did I? No, we're friends and that's all that matters. Now, do you have anything else you want to tell me or are we going to finish this shitty movie you wanted to watch?"

Most of the people I came out to over this period were my closest friends, while I came out to some people based on necessity. One example would be my manager.

I was in a long-distance relation with someone in Ōamaru, which is roughly four hours south of Ōtautahi. I had no transport options besides the intercity bus as I was still on my learner's licence. I needed my manager's permission to modify my roster to accommodate the bus schedule. It was difficult for me to gauge whether it was safe for me to come out because there were few visibly Queer people in the office. The few Queer people were all based in Te Whanganui-a-Tara. My greatest concern was whether the news of my coming out would travel back to my family. Aotearoa is a small country after all, and we often joke about our "two degrees of separation".

"Can I talk to you in private?" I approached my manager while he was tapping away on his Surface Pro at his desk. I finally mustered the courage within me to tell him.

"Of course," my manager replied. He was surprised by my sudden request. "Should we find a meeting room?"

Oh no. My manager must have thought I was going to hand in my resignation. He led me to a meeting room. I quickly scanned the office as I shut the door. The walls of our meeting rooms were notoriously thin.

"I need to tell you something," and I told my manager what I had rehearsed in my head all morning.

"Thank you for sharing that with me," my manager replied. He let out a massive sigh of relief. "Is there anything I can do for you?"

We continued talking in the meeting room. We talked about personal development. We were also talking about how we could continue promoting our services to *hapū, iwi,* and Māori. In the back of my mind, I was now out of the closet in a professional environment. Unpredictably, it was through my work and my connection with *takatāpui* that helped me advance on my coming out journey.

I was in Tāmaki Makaurau for work, and I was staying with Amit. I had met with Ashish for dinner the night before. I had an uneasy night's sleep as I struggled to digest the Thai food from the Albert Street Asian Food Hall.

Peter picked me up from Amit's apartment in the central city. He is a well-known and well-spoken *takatāpui* advocate and lawyer. He was a few years my senior and he was working as an advisor. It was just us on the road. We were on the way to Kirikiriroa (Hamilton) to facilitate a series of *hui* (meetings) with local iwi.

"Mind if I play some music?" Peter asked me as he connected his phone to the car. *Girls Like You* began playing through the car stereo.

"What's your background?" Peter asked me as we drove past Raahui Pookeka (Huntly). "How did you manage to get this fancy role anyway?"

Peter was suspicious about my intentions. And rightfully so. Why would someone with no *Māori whakapapa* (genealogy) be in a role providing a service to hapu, iwi, and Māori?

"I was desperate for work after I finished my master's. I was at the Inland Revenue before this, and it seemed like a better option than processing GST returns." I told him honestly. There was no point for me in lying. "I applied for the role because I have a background working with data in linguistics and I studied some *te reo Māori* (Māori language) at university."

"Linguistics." Peter savoured the word. He kept his eyes on the road and continued his volley of questions. "What was your topic?"

"I was looking into the vocal satisfaction of transmasculine and non-binary people," I replied.

I was not sure how much to tell him.

"Oh." Something I said had piqued Peter' interest. "Are you trans or Queer?" "No," I responded, wondering what Peter would ask next. "I'm an ally, I guess."

"Sounds interesting." Peter was deep in thought. "What's the application of your research?"

I summarised the findings of my research. I talked about how we could apply my findings in a clinical setting to support transmasculine and non-binary people. I went into extreme detail on how gender as a social construct influences the way we use language.

"How interesting." Peter sounded impressed with my answer.

"Can you tell me about your culture? How do your beliefs influence the way you view gender?" As we drove through the King Country, I told Peter how my culture is a synthesis of different belief systems and how the social manifestation of 三 教 (*saam¹gaau³*; the three teachings) influenced my perspectives of sexuality and gender. He was fascinated; and he attempted to draw parallels between our different world views.

"Why is this first time I've heard about this?" Peter asked me as we reached our destination. "Many Cantonese or Chinese in Aotearoa don't follow this way of life anymore," I answered Peter honestly. "We were told we had to assimilate if we wanted to succeed." "You mean assimilate to Pākehā whiteness?" Peter interjected.

I nodded at Peter's interpretation. I felt disheartened and defeated.

As we drove back to Tāmaki Makaurau following our meetings, I sat in the passenger seat feeling uneasy. I felt a sense of sadness acknowledging the eventual dissolution of my culture. If I could no longer be Cantonese or be Queer, what was left of my identity?

"I need to be honest with you," I confessed to Peter. "I lied. I'm not an ally. I'm gay." "Are you okay?" Peter asked me. "Are you out to your family?"

"I'm not out to my family yet," I replied. "I don't know how. I'm scared."

"Sidney, don't be scared." Peter reassured me. "If you can safely come out to your family then you should. You must share your experience for those who don't have the luxury to be their true authentic selves."

At this point, the indigestion from the Thai food I had had the night before developed into a bought of food poisoning. I asked Peter to pull over as I began to vomit on the side of the road.

All I knew when I went back to Ōtautahi was that I needed to come out to my parents.

Letting in
Te Awakairangi, Spring 2019

Not long after my conversation with Peter, I was once again back in Te Whanganui-a-Tara. I was there for work, and Peter wanted to see me before I went home that night.

"Promise me you'll talk to your parents," Peter told me when we met. "Only if you're ready." I was going to be there for two days. Initially, I was going to be selfish. I was going to come out to my parents at the airport, but I knew I needed to give my parents some time to process their feelings about my identity.

My commute home was fuelled with anxiety. I knew I had to come out to my parents that night, but I did not know how and when. As the train pulled up at my station, Dad was there to pick me up. Mum was not in the car as she was at home preparing dinner. As we pulled into the driveway, I saw Mum cooking in the garage. Like most Cantonese parents, Mum's love language was food.

"Not now," I thought to myself.

「我返屋企啦.」 (I'm home!) I yelled from the car. Our usual routine.

「返屋企啦，就食得飯. 快去洗手. 無唔記得裝香.」 (You're home, dinner's nearly ready. Go wash your hands. Don't forget to offer.) She instructed me from the garage.

I did as I was told. I washed my hands and then I offered incense to the Ancestors. After that, I set the table. As we sat down around the table, I could see from Mum's expression that she was happy that I was finally home. I noticed that she had cooked my favourite dishes.

"Not now," I thought. Mum would not forgive me if I ruined dinner.

「食飯啦.」 (Let's eat) We said in unison as we dug into our meal.

Mum was busy chatting in the background. I was not hungry at all. The only thing going through my mind was when I was going to come out to her. I picked at the dishes with my chopsticks. Intrusive thoughts fuelled my growing anxiety.

"How was I going to tell Mum?"

"Was this meal the last time I would experience Mum's cooking?"

After dinner, I went to my room, and I laid down on my bed. I was restless. I was flooded with memories from my childhood. Numerous questions raced through my mind.

"How many more lies did I want to tell?"

"How many more secrets did I need to keep from my family?"

I reflected on the conversation I had had with Peter.

"You need to harness your privilege. Share your stories so those who can't tell their stories can also be heard."

I knew my parents tolerated my uncle's Queer identity. I was in no immediate danger. Furthermore, I had housing and financial security if things did go wrong. There were no reasons for me not to come out besides rejection. If acceptance was not attainable immediately, then tolerance would have to do for now.

"I'm going to do it," I messaged Peter.

"Good luck. Take care," Peter texted back.

I got up from my bed and I trudged to the kitchen. Each step was laden with guilt. Mum was washing the dishes.

「不如去練車啦.」 (How about we go for a drive?) I asked Mum.

「好呀.」 (Sounds good.) Mum responded and dried her hands.

It was late spring, and the days were starting to get longer. Mum put in a CD of classic Cantonese songs as we backed out of the driveway.

I knew Mum had a lot she wanted to say to me. My cousin was staying with us at the time and there was a lot she did not want to say in the house. I sat there listening to her, driving down the now empty high street. I was still debating in my head when and how I should tell Mum. I wanted to tell her first so she could then tell Dad. I really did not know how he would react.

I followed the path that was laid out before me. I parked up the car by the beach overlooking the harbour. The sun was setting beyond the western hills. The sky was lit orange and red. It was in that moment that I came out to Mum. My hands gripped the steering wheel. My shoulders tensed and I hoped for the worst.

「你唔會介意如果我鍾意男人呀.」 (You won't mind if I like men, right?) I asked Mum. Mum's expression told me she was deep in thought. She looked away into the distance, before she let out a massive sigh. She finally replied after what felt like a lifetime.

「雖然我覺得唔正常, 但係我唔理你鍾意邊個最緊要佢對你係真心.」 (Even though I don't think it's normal, I don't care who you like as long as their feelings for you are real.) Mum replied with teary eyes.

I could tell Mum was in shock, but at least my anxiety was gone as I had achieved what I had aimed to do. All I could do was reflect on Mum's words as we drove away. We stopped by Countdown on the way home and I bought a tiramisu. I knew I would not get acceptance, but tolerance was more than I expected. We did not talk much after that.

"It's done. Thank you," I messaged Peter when I got home.

「我話咗俾你個阿爸聽啦.」 (I've spoken to your Dad.) Mum told me the next day.

I heard a hint of disappointment in Mum's voice. We were on our way to the airport. I knew she had only told me now as she did not want to say anything within earshot of my cousin.

「咁我啲孫呢.」 (But what about our grandchildren?) Dad had asked me innocently.

I could tell that my parents were in grief. They were grieving for a vision they had for me that would not come to fruition. I knew that my parents felt like they had let down our Ancestors, as they knew I would not be the one to provide grandchildren or to extend our family line. They blamed themselves for raising a culturally deficient child. After all their efforts uprooting themselves from their home and migrating to Aotearoa, this was what they got to show for it. I knew they saw me as a failure. Single-handedly I had shattered their dream. I knew it would take time for them to come to terms with their grief. We drove in silence to the airport.

When I finally landed in Ōtautahi, I broke the news to my flatmates about my coming out. In contrast to the sombre reaction of my parents, my flatmates got me a Rainbow cake to celebrate the occasion. The day I came out to my parents was Tuesday, 20 November 2018, which was exactly one year after I had submitted my thesis. When I came out to my parents, I expected it to be the end of my coming out journey, but it was only the beginning.

Content warning

This chapter contains references to abuse; hateful behaviour directed at religious groups; homophobia; mental illness and ableism; nudity; racism and racial slurs; self-harm and suicidal thoughts, intentions, and actions; substance use and abuse; swear words or curse words; and violence.

The chapter starts overleaf.

9
to long for a memory

Ōtautahi, Spring 2016

It was the night of the Kaikōura earthquake. I was with Ashish and Akhil in their flat. We were sitting around the hookah and drinking beer when the earth came to life two minutes after midnight. The flat creaked and slowly evolved into a low rumble. The furniture rattled around us. I kept a close eye on the TV as it rocked from side to side.

"I better head back," I told Ashish and Akhil as I made my way to the door.

I wanted to check on my flatmates who were living down the road. An earthquake at this magnitude meant potential aftershocks and tsunamis. I would rather be home if we were instructed to evacuate or go to higher ground. Thankfully, we were relatively safe in Ōtautahi with most of the damage reported in Te Whanganui-a-Tara. I was in bed reading updates on my phone when I received an unexpected message.

"Are you still awake?" Rakim asked me in the message. "I'm scared."

I had met Rakim a few weeks earlier on Grindr. He had a blank profile with no username or photos. All he had was a photo of a crumpled red duvet.

"Hi." This was my introduction to Rakim.

I wanted to be polite. After exchanging a few messages, Rakim finally reciprocated with some photos. If the photos were anything to go by, he was incredibly handsome. He had dark wavy hair, big brown eyes, and a strong jawline. Everything about him was perfectly sculpted.

"What do you do?" Rakim asked me.

"I study linguistics," I told Rakim. "On the vocal satisfaction of transmasculine people." "Oh," Rakim responded. I sensed confusion. "I'm studying too."

I did not expect him to know much about my field of study, but our conversation did not flow either. He eventually revealed more about himself the more time we spent talking.

"I'm from Kerala," Rakim told me. "I'm also doing a master's degree at Lincoln University." I later found out Rakim only told me a half-truth. It was a postgraduate diploma. Conveniently, he lived near me on Middleton Road.

"Do you want to meet up?" I asked out of curiosity.

"No, I just want someone to talk to," Rakim responded. "It's lonely being an international student in New Zealand. I should go now. I've got work tomorrow."

"Nice talking to you then." I wished him good night and then I went to sleep.

"Do you want me to come over?" I asked Rakim following his message. The earth came to life once again as we experienced an aftershock. I did not know what else to do.

"Yes. Can you?" Rakim replied, and he sent me his address.

I waited until my flatmates had gone to their rooms before I snuck out of the flat. Rakim was standing there in his pyjamas on Middleton Road.

"Hi! You must be Rakim," I greeted the stranger.

Rakim made a gesture to tell me to be quiet. He led me down the driveway, and we hurried towards a unit. He carefully unlocked the door and once again made a gesture to instruct me to be quiet. I guess he did not want to wake up the others in the unit.

I made my way towards Rakim's bedroom and moments later, I was lying there in his single bed in silence. What was I doing? I hardly knew him, and I was lying in his bed.

I brought my arm around and held Rakim for a while in the dark. I kissed him, but I felt no spark. We spent the night together anyway. The next morning, I was still in his bed.

"We need to stay here until they leave," Rakim whispered in my ear. He pointed at the door.

I was lying there in a small stuffy room. I was next to a stranger I had only met the night before. We lay there listening to the sound of a young family getting ready for their day. It was midday before we finally heard the door slam shut – silence.

"Okay," Rakim whispered. "Let me check if they're gone."

Rakim got up and left the room. A few seconds later, he poked his head through the door. We were now free to leave his room. He took me to the kitchen. He stood there in his underwear in front of the stove. When it was ready, he handed me a mug of *chaya*.

"They're North Indian," Rakim told me. "They don't know I'm on Grindr."

Rakim and I stood there in silence sipping away at our mugs of *chaya*. He spiced the beverage with pods of cardamom.

"I should go to work now," Rakim announced as he knocked back his *chaya*.

Rakim took my mug from me, washed it, and put mine away back in the cupboard while he placed his in the sink. I realised that he did not want his flatmates to know that he had brought a guest over. I would later come to learn that he was not actually scared; he was just in need of company. That evening set the precedent for our relationship. Little did I know that he was going to play a major role in my life over the next few years.

Unsettled boundaries
Ōtautahi, Summer 2016

What was supposed to be a chance encounter turned into a routine. Rakim worked split shifts at a kebab shop. I would wait for him until he finished his morning shift. I would wait with him at a cafe until his evening shift began. Sometimes he would come to my flat. I would sneak him into my room. I did not know why he needed discretion since I was already out to my flatmates.

"Can you help me with my CV?" Rakim asked me one day. "I keep getting rejected."

Rakim needed a job related to his degree to apply for residency. I agreed to help him. As I continued to help him, I grew fond of his company. I began to develop feelings for him. The more time we spent together, the more he told me of his story.

"Dad wants me to get married," Rakim told me. "My parents don't know I'm gay."

Rakim used study as an excuse to escape, but moving to Aotearoa was not a simple feat. He had received a scholarship of ₹20,000, but that was not enough. He had convinced his mum to remortgage her house with the bank to borrow a further ₹ 2,100,000. I was stunned when he told me that the annual interest was 15 per cent.

"This is my favourite movie," Rakim told me as we watched *Dostana* (2008) from my laptop. The movie was a Queer-coded buddy comedy. I could tell Rakim saw himself in those characters even though it was fiction. We paused the movie several times, as we made out in my bed.

"I don't know what I would do without you," Rakim told me as he kissed me on the lips.

The more I learnt about Rakim, the more I learnt about his family and his friends back home. I lived vicariously through his stories to learn what it is like to be Queer in Kerala.

"My best friend Advik works as a fashion designer," Rakim told me one afternoon when I asked him if he had any gay friends back home.

"We met online. I nearly walked out on our 'our' date when I realised that he had edited his photos. Anyway, I gave him a chance because I needed him to take me home on his scooter."

Rakim and Advik were open about their friendship, but neither of their parents knew they were gay. Unlike Rakim, Advik did not have the same excuse. He did not have the money to leave the country.

"Advik's getting married," Rakim later informed me.

"Advik? Really? To whom?" I was surprised by the news.

Of the few times I spoke to Advik, he was not interested in getting married at all.

"She's a university lecturer," Rakim told me while he scrolled through his phone uninterested. "She teaches economics. It doesn't matter. He's only doing it to please his mum."

"It's good news. It means he doesn't need to hide about sleeping with men anymore," Rakim continued. He sounded happy for Advik. "His mum won't care as long as they have children."

Rakim saw my expression and put down his phone. I was in disbelief.

Rakim told me that for many of his friends, getting married was their only route to freedom. They fulfilled their obligations once they were married. They were then free to do whatever they wanted. I knew that this was great news for Advik. What about his wife? Was this our future?

With the limited time we had together between his shifts and my commitments at the university, our main mode of communication was through food. Rakim made me beef fry, *idli, wada,* and *sambar.* I made him classic Cantonese dishes – without pork.

"I'll teach you how to make beef fry," Rakim proposed one morning. "This is my favourite dish, but I can only eat this when I'm with Dad".

Rakim's father was Muslim, and his mother was Hindu. Naturally, his grandparents disapproved of the relationship. His parents fought fiercely for their relationship to be recognised by the family. Eventually, his parents ran away and had Rakim in secret.

The situation got better until it got worse, and Rakim's parents eventually separated. His dad remarried a Muslim woman and moved to Sharjah for work. His mum was still alone in Kerala. Some love stories were not meant to last.

"Cut the beef into cubes," Rakim instructed me while he closely observed me from the counter. "Get the pressure cooker, and with the meat, put in two cinnamon quills, two bay leaves, two pods of star anise three cloves, four cardamom pods, ginger, garlic paste, meat masala."

"The masala must be from Kerala otherwise it won't taste right," Rakim interjected quickly. "Finally, some black pepper powder, coriander powder, turmeric powder, chilli powder, salt, fresh mint, and some yoghurt to tenderise the meat."

As I followed Rakim's instructions, I felt a sense of security. At home, we were just like a regular couple, but in public we had to mask our relationship.

"This is my friend," Rakim introduced me at his graduation. "He's just my neighbour." "Don't tell anyone we're together," Rakim instructed me. "And don't talk about what you're studying. They might suspect something."

As the ceremony progressed, the number of Rakim's classmates asking about my connection increased. Eventually, it became too much. I felt like an imposter. I found a quiet spot near the library and had a panic attack.

"What are you doing?" Rakim asked me when he found me alone sitting on the stone steps. "We should go back. My classmates will be looking for me."

There were times when our values would clash.

"I don't want you to hang out with the North Indians anymore," Rakim shouted at me one afternoon. He had found out that I had been with Ashish and Akhil. It was one of our first and only fight.

"You need to choose between me or those North Indians," Rakim continued. "You don't understand. They're a bad influence on you."

"What's wrong with spending time with my friends?" I asked Rakim innocently.

"I don't like it when you're with them," Rakim argued. "You're just wasting your time." "But they're my friends," I cried in desperation.

"Why do you want to hurt me? Do you want me to kill myself?" Rakim threatened me. I knew this was rhetorical.

"I'm going home. I'll let you decide," Rakim announced before he stormed out of the room.

I was scared. It was not the first time that I had experienced Rakim's rage. A few days earlier, we had been out for dinner, and I had been unimpressed with him. He had spent the whole evening on his phone.

"Why are you always on your phone?" I told Rakim as we got in the car.

"It's because I miss home. You won't understand. I need to know what's happening with my friends," Rakim barked at me.

"We're on a date, we're supposed to talk," I told Rakim. "Pull over. I'll walk home."

I watched Rakim grip the steering wheel. Rakim put his foot on the accelerator and sped down Suva Street before he came to an immediate stop.

My heart raced as I began to panic. I lost control of my body as I broke down in tears and I began to hyperventilate. I was having a panic attack.

Rakim realised what he had done and tried to soothe me.

"Don't let your flatmates see you like this," Rakim instructed me as he led me into my flat. I dried my tears and slowed down my breathing. I put on a smile as I greeted my flatmates. When Rakim stormed out of my room after our argument, I sat in my room alone. I remembered how I felt when Jono tried to kill himself. I did not want to go through the same situation again. I complied with his request.

"Where have you been?" Akhil asked me. This was the last time I saw him before he moved to Tāmaki Makaurau. "Ashish said you stopped replying to his messages."

"I'm sorry. I've just been super busy," I lied.

"Can we still hang out?" Akhil responded with a hint of disappointment. "Is there something you're not telling us?"

"No," I lied again.

To this day, I still regret how I treated my friends.

Long distance
Ōamaru, Autumn 2016

"I have a job offer!" Rakim told me excitedly. "I start in two weeks."

After weeks of searching, Rakim was finally offered a job at a dairy processing plant near Ōamaru. I was excited for him as it meant he was one step closer to applying for residency.

"I want you to help me," Rakim requested. "Can you come with me to Ōamaru?" "Okay," I agreed hesitantly. I was beginning to fall behind on my master's coursework.

The next two weeks was a mad dash. I found him a car and helped him pack. The only thing missing was a place to live in Ōamaru. Unfortunately, there were few options in Ōamaru, so we ended up in Waimate.

"My partner and I are looking for a place close to his work," I told the property manager.

The property manager was showing us around the flat. It was a unit across the road from the iconic St Patrick's Basilica. Rakim glared at me.

"This is a great option," the property manager told us as she showed us around. "It's a short walk from the town and the plant is just down the road. You and your partner will be happy here."

"Why did you say that?" Rakim scolded me as we got back to the car. There was a tenseness in his voice. "We need to look somewhere else now. What if she knows someone from the plant?"

After three days in Ōamaru, we were still unsuccessful in finding Rakim any accommodation. There were limited options and the places available were either too expensive or too damp. Some of the rentals looking for flatmates were not receptive to his presence.

Every night, we shifted to a different motel. Rakim was paranoid that the motel owners would suspect we were a couple.

It was Rakim's first day at work and we were still struggling to find him accommodation. I spent his first day alone in the motel. The room was cold but overlooked the port and the harbour. I watched the seagulls on the breakwater and dreamt of a day when I no longer needed to lie.

We finally found Rakim a place to stay on the fourth day. We found a room for board with a young Pakistani family. They were happy for him to move in immediately. Relief.

"Will you be back soon?" Rakim asked me as he dropped me off at the bus stop. "Of course," I responded confidently. "We'll make it work."

We took turns visiting each other in the first few months. Rakim was still paranoid, so every visit we stayed at a different motel. We would request two or more beds and on check-out, we ruffled the bed sheets to "trick" the owners.

"We can't keep doing this," I told Rakim as I was waiting for my bus back to Ōtautahi. "We can't afford to pay for a motel every time I came to visit. We need to get you your own place."

Thankfully, I found Rakim a one-bedroom apartment. This time I did not make the mistake of revealing our relationship to the real estate agent.

When we finally moved into the one-bedroom apartment, we had a brief moment of normality. This was before Rakim found out that a colleague lived in a neighbouring unit.

"Keep the curtains closed," Rakim instructed me. "I don't want the neighbours to know that we're sleeping in the same bed."

Rakim decided our only option was to leave Ōamaru when I was there. As soon as I arrived, we hopped into his car, and we spent hours on the road. We drove between rural towns and hoped that we did not know anyone there. I felt like we were on the run. But then again, what were we running from?

"I need you. I don't know what I'd do with my life if we weren't together," Rakim told me one night as we were in bed. We were in Takapō (Lake Tekapo).

"Don't be silly," I comforted Rakim. "Why'd you say something like that?"

"I'm serious," Rakim replied. "I'd kill myself if we were no longer together."

Between 2017 and 2019, I took over forty bus trips between Ōtautahi and Ōamaru. I spent over 20,000 kilometres on the road, which is the equivalent distance from Aotearoa to India and back. One Christmas Eve, I took a bus down to Ōamaru in the morning and returned to Ōtautahi on the same day. Rakim forgot to tell me that he had volunteered for the Christmas shift. After all, he did not have any family in Aotearoa. I finally got home at ten minutes to midnight.

I saw a lot of Te Waipounamu during this time. I also had a lot of time to reflect on my identity during those journeys up and down the plains of Waitaha. He held my hand as he drove. This was the only time I experienced any physical intimacy in public.

I never told my family about my relationship with Rakim. I pretended I was in Ōtautahi when I was in Ōamaru. I became paranoid that they would discover my lies, so I disabled the geolocation function on my phone. I also stopped posting updates on my social media. My life was dictated by the bus schedule, and my social life soon suffered.

As our relationship progressed, it became more one-sided. When the university invited me to graduate with my master's degree, I gave Rakim advance notice so he could apply for leave. I told my family not to come for my graduation, as he did not want my family to be there.

"I can't ask for time off," Rakim told me days before the event. "It's too late."

"I asked you months ago," I responded angrily. "Don't come. I don't want to beg anymore."

It became quite clear that Rakim was not interested in coming to Ōtautahi. In hindsight, I wonder if all the time I spent on the road was worth it.

Letting go
Ōtautahi, Spring 2019

As I continued to live a double life between Ōamaru and Ōtautahi, my Queer identity flourished as I attended more Queer events. My first FriGay was both a liberating and terrifying experience. Christchurch Pride at Pegasus Arms on Oxford Terrace hosted it.

These temporary spaces enabled our Queer communities to come together and express themselves in a safe environment. One event led to another, and I attended my first local drag show hosted by Over the Rainbow which headlined Holy Fuq, Nytmare, and Lady Bubbles. I was in awe of how the Queer scene in Ōtautahi had developed since coming out.

"You shouldn't be going to those kinds of events," Rakim commented when he found out I was going to FriGay. "I thought you were educated enough to make better decisions."

I was numb to Rakim's hollow threats, and my yearning for a sense of community outweighed his unrealistic expectations. If he genuinely cared about me, then he would be in Ōtautahi. I stopped telling Rakim when I attended these events.

I discovered the importance of being part of a wider community even though I felt intimidated as a visual minority in these spaces. When I was in Ōtautahi, I was free to live my life as an openly Queer person, but when I was in Ōamaru, I was back in the closet.

"You need to be honest with yourself," Peter advised me when I saw him. I was in Te Whanganui-a-Tara for work, and he wanted to know how I was after coming out to my parents. "What you have isn't a relationship. You need to learn to let go and do what's best for you."

Another benefit of being part of a community was that I began to see examples of what it meant to be in a healthy relationship. What we had was not a healthy relationship as Rakim was deliberately keeping me in the closet.

Since the terrorist attacks in Ōtautahi, Rakim had only made one trip to Ōtautahi. I was exhausted with the travelling, and I resented my trips to Ōamaru. As per his request, I moved into a single-room apartment, as he felt unsafe around my flatmates. I thought this would be enough for him to feel a sense of security.

Nevertheless, Rakim continued to make excuses. He told me he had no intention of coming out, but he was unhappy for me to be involved with the wider Queer community. He began to threaten me by weaponising his body. He tried to manipulate my emotions as he had done at the start of our turbulent relationship. What we had was a toxic relationship.

"Why do you keep hurting me?" Rakim accused me. "You really want me to kill myself?" It became clear our relationship was untenable.

On my final trip to Ōamaru, I knew what I had to do. I was ready to turn my back on the closet we had built together in that town.

"Will I see you next weekend?" Rakim asked me.

"Of course," I lied to him.

I gave him one last kiss and boarded the bus – one last time. It was spring of 2019. I looked beyond the farmland and watched as lightning lit up Ka Kirikiri o te Moana (Southern Alps). The bus was empty. It was just the driver and me on this the empty stretch of road. I was free.

"We're done," I told Rakim the next day.

"Why would you say something like this?" Rakim asked me. "You're trying to kill me?"

I continued to receive a barrage of messages from Rakim. He texted, emailed, and sent messages on Facebook, WhatsApp, and LinkedIn. Notification after notification. I blocked every message and each time he would find another way to contact me. I found breaking up with Rakim harder than coming out to my parents. Fortunately, I had distance on my side, but I lived in constant fear as he had keys to my one-bedroom apartment.

"Can I talk to you?" Rakim begged me. "Can I see you?"

One time I received an unexpected deposit in my bank account. It was from Rakim. "Talk to me," it said in the reference column of the transaction.

Shortly after, I started seeing Jake. We met playing touch rugby with the Christchurch Heroes. "Just wondering if you'd like your keys back today?" Rakim asked me in an email. He had found my work email address. "I'm in Christchurch. If you can meet me in the city, I can hand them over to you. Please let me know or else I'll leave."

I ignored the email as I predicted Rakim would use my keys as a bargaining chip.

"Can you stay with me tonight? I think Rakim is in town, and I'm scared he might turn up unannounced," I asked Jake.

Like clockwork, Jake and I were on the couch watching Coast versus Country when I heard a knock on the window. It was Rakim.

"Hi!" Rakim shouted excitedly. He waved at me through the sheer curtains.

Rakim's expression changed from excitement to fear when Jake sat up from the couch. He walked away. That was the last time I saw him in person, but the contact continued.

"We have a package for you," the receptionist alerted me. I was not expecting mail.

I went downstairs and the receptionist handed me a white package. I tossed it between my hands. There were no return to sender details, but I had an idea. I unwrapped it carefully when I got back to my desk. Relief. It was just a Coca Cola bottle with "Siddie Sid" on the label.

"Just wondering if you got my present?" Rakim asked on LinkedIn. Block.

My last interaction with Rakim came through the mail.

"I hope you are doing well. I'm requesting help," Rakim asked in an email. He had found my university email address. "I'm going through a bad phase in my life, and I need some mental support. I need to talk to someone. You are the only one who I can talk to openly. Please consider me as a friend and talk to me? I do not have many friends. It is a lot of stress being away from my family. I feel like I am at a point where my mental health is about to crumble. Can we please talk as friends?"

I deleted the email. I felt heartless, but I had to do what was best for me. He was no longer my responsibility. I went home, gathered Rakim's things, and posted them to him the next day.

"You did the right thing. It's not your responsibility to be part of his coming out journey," my therapist told me afterwards. "A partner is there to support you; instead, he's become dependent on you. It's not your job to fix him. It's not your job to be a saviour, Sidney."

Slowly, I reconnected with my friends. I apologised to Ashish and Akhil. I am grateful for those who stood by me as I rebuilt my life. My greatest regret is that my family still do not know about this chapter of my life. I hope after reading this they will forgive me.

Content warning

This chapter contains references to death, dying, and mass murder; homophobia; mental illness and ableism; racism and racial slurs; self-harm and suicidal thoughts, intentions, and actions; swear words or curse words; transphobia; and violence.

The chapter starts overleaf.

10

to inherit the teachings of one's forebears

Ōtautahi, Winter 2019

It was a Friday night; Molly and I were sitting on one of the cardboard pews at the Transitional Cathedral. The cathedral was meant to be a temporary structure while the Christchurch Cathedral, which was severely damaged in the 2010–2011 earthquakes, was being repaired. We affectionately called it the Cardboard Cathedral.

Molly and I were not there for a church service. We were there waiting for a drag show to begin. This was the complete opposite of what most people would expect from a city with a name like Christchurch. The theme of the night was Broadway musicals. As I waited for the show to begin, I reflected on my personal journey so far and the distance I had made coming out. I observed the crowd around me, and it made me realise the progress that had been made in increasing Queer visibility since I had first stepped foot in this city.

It might be a surprise to most people that this unremarkable city was a key location in Aotearoa's journey towards Queer liberation. Unfortunately, what sparked this paradigmatic shift was the murder of Charles Arthur Allen Aberhart in 1964 (Skews-Poole, 2017). Allen, which was the name he preferred, was brutally beaten to death in Hagley Park by six teenagers who set out that night to "to belt up a Queer". A visitor from Waiharakeke (Blenheim), he unknowingly went cruising in Hagley Park, which was then known for incidents of "Queer bashing".

The perpetrators were arrested the following day, and a jury acquitted all six teenagers after five days of trial. The only mention decrying homophobia was in the judge's statement: "The man who died might have had homosexual tendencies, but he had a right to live." The case received minimal media coverage, but word of the senseless murder and the injustice in Ōtautahi became a rallying cry for the gay and lesbian communities across Aotearoa.

This incident set into motion what would be a two-decade long journey towards homosexual law reform. In the sixty years since the brutal murder, there is still little acknowledgement of Allen's sacrifice. We must learn from history in order to avoid these same mistakes in the future. With the city's dark past coupled with its reputation as "the most racist city in New Zealand", it is no wonder many Queer people still choose to avoid Ōtautahi.

While I learnt how to navigate this new physical closet, only a few people at work knew about my Queer identity. Molly was one of my best friends at work and we were inseparable. I jokingly described her as my work spouse. She was one of the few that knew that I was in a closeted relationship and knew about my continued struggles of being in the closet at work. We are still remarkably close now even though we no longer work together.

"We have to go!" I told her. "This is a once in a lifetime opportunity. When else are we going to see a drag show … in a church!"

Just a few weeks earlier, I had attended another drag show at Little Neighbourhood bar on Victoria Street. The theme was "Drag it Back to the 80s". Only a few weeks earlier, I was still technically in the closet. I went alone, and I sat by myself alone at the back of the bar nursing my pint of Speight's. I watched a local drag artist, Nyte Mare, lip sync to Mariah.

I felt silly being there. I did not know what it meant to be a Queer person or how to express my Queerness. After spending nearly twenty-five years hiding my true self, I felt lost with my identity.

I did not know what it meant to be my authentic self.

This time it was different. By this point, I had already come out to my family. I was no longer worried that I would accidentally out myself in public. I no longer had to scrutinise my every activity on social media. I felt a sense of liberation sitting there in the cathedral waiting for the drag artists to perform to a sold-out crowd.

The lights dimmed, and the audience fell silent. The cardboard cross on the wall was backlit with a green spotlight. Smoke billowed on to the stage.

"This is it!" I told Molly eagerly. "Let the show begin!"

Out at work
Ōtautahi, Spring 2018

Before I came out, I was already part of the diversity and inclusion working group at work. I found it difficult to contribute to the working group, when I had to filter everything I had to say with the fear that I would give myself away as Queer.

"I don't understand what the big deal is about coming out," the chief people officer once loudly announced during a working group meeting. "I've had to come out to my mates when I told them I liked football more than rugby. It's just about preference, isn't it."

Senior leadership frequently made flippant remarks like this. These diversity and inclusion initiatives were just a facade.

When I finally came out, I quickly realised that there was an absence of Queer representation at work. While this worked to my advantage when I was still in the closet, it did not help when I wanted to form a community. Naturally, I wanted to use my lived experience to ensure that everyone at work could be their authentic selves.

My initial goal was to establish an informal social network for Queer staff. I took stock of the Queer people at work. This was not an easy task. There were few people who were openly Queer in the public service – let alone our office in Ōtautahi.

"Why would anyone want to come out in a place like this?" I would think to myself.

"Would you like to help me form a Rainbow Network in the office?" I asked Hannah one Friday afternoon. She had told me she was bisexual at another after-work drinks and I thought she would be the best person to ask first.

"How did you know?" she responded in shock. Hannah was surprised by my question.

"Don't you remember?" I told her. I was quite confident I did not imagine this interaction. "You told me you're bisexual."

"Oh, really?" she was clearly trying hard to remember when she came out to me. "I thought it was something I had done."

"Nah," I laughed at her. "I've got a pretty dysfunctional gaydar."

"You're right, that really doesn't make any sense," Hannah seemed a bit more relaxed now. "I guess it won't hurt for us to start a network and see where it goes."

We started by organising a discreet morning tea at a bar across the road from the office. The Rockpool was a self-described gastropub, but it was honestly more of a dive bar. *Tradies* (trades people) would come in for a cheeky pint of beer after a hard morning of work.

We assembled a small group of people who were out in the office. As we sat in the dingy bar, we drafted the purpose of our network, and what we wanted to achieve. Over time, our network slowly grew into an expanding mailing list as more Queer people wanted to connect with other Queer people in the office. We devised strategies to invite people discreetly. We would include each email address as equipment so it would not be so obvious in the calendar. As our network grew, our meetings became more frequent, and our purpose became more transparent.

We wanted greater visibility of our Queer communities; we identified the lack of accessible spaces; we wanted a transparent transition at work policy; and we wanted a greater say in how our organisation engaged with our Queer communities. More and more Queer people began to join us from across the country.

"I didn't even realise we had a Rainbow community here," a senior staff member told me one day over a cup of coffee. She had been in the organisation for over a decade. "We've always been here, but we've just never had a space to create a community."

We realised we had become complacent with tolerance, but we were still far from acceptance. Some of us were comfortable with the status quo when there was still a need to advocate for our transgender and non-binary communities.

"Do we include allies?" became the recurring question at our meetings. Our initial stance was that Queer spaces were for Queer people, but I did not have to look too far into the past to see the hypocrisy of this belief. I too once heavily relied on my role as an ally and an outside observer to navigate my Queer identity. I realised that I did not want to be the gatekeeper.

Being part of a network gave me the opportunity to connect with and learn from Queer people throughout the country. I met Dan who was a human resources adviser. I was surprised when he made me realise that I was affected by the ethnic pay gap.

"I have spoken to your manager, and I told him he has one of two choices," Dan told me excitedly on the phone. "He can admit that he's racist or homophobic if he doesn't do anything about your salary. You should get a salary review letter soon."

Dan also made me realise the inequities experienced by ethnic and gender minorities in the public service. I could not thank him enough for advocating on my behalf. He is still a remarkably close friend of mine to this day.

As I turned my focus towards myself, the network flourished and developed into a fully-fledged employee-led network with funding from the organisation.

Holding out for a hero
Ōtautahi, Spring 2018

"You look like someone who can handle a ball," Ritchie asked me jokingly while we were in the tearoom eating lunch. "I'm organising touch rugby this year. Would you be interested in joining the Standard Deviants? We play at South Hagley."

For the uninitiated, rugby has attained a religious status in Aotearoa. Many kids grew up playing a version of rugby: ripper, touch, union, or league. Neither of my parents saw the benefit of contact sports, so I was not involved in any rugby at all. The first time I handled a rugby ball was in October 2018 with the Standard Deviants.

I was an awful player, but I was glad Ritchie had asked me to join the Standard Deviants. Little would I realise that a sense of Queer liberation would come to me in the form of a rugby ball. Fast forward to September 2019, I was at FriGay night drinks at the Pegasus Arms on Oxford Terrace. At that point in time, I had left my abusive relationship and I was free to go wherever I wanted without guilt.

I was at a bar leaner with Owen and Hannah when a stranger approached me. He tapped me on the shoulder. He was wearing a shirt with a massive Rainbow across his chest.

"Hey, how's it going? I'm Nathan," Nathan asked me as he handed me a flyer for the Christchurch Heroes. "Have you played touch rugby before?"

"I've tried playing for my work team, but I'm not any good at it," I told him. I took the flyer from him nervously.

"You should play for us then. We're not any good either, but we have fun," he replied jokingly. "I'll see you at training then!"

Nathan smiled and then waved at me before walking away to the next group of people. I examined the flyer: "Christchurch Heroes, a collective of LGBTI+ inclusive sport teams which aim to empower the Rainbow community, and their whanau, to engage in sports and activities."

"You should give it a go. What have you got to lose?" Owen told me as he returned to his pint. He seemed unfazed by the interaction.

I put the flyer away, and I went back to my pint. I could sense that this was going to be another fateful coincidence.

I tossed and turned on the idea for weeks before I finally built up the confidence to attend training. I biked from the university to Westminster Park in Mairehau. As I reached the field, I felt my heart pounding in my chest.

"You must be Rawiri," I said as I got off my bike. I had sent him an email a few days earlier. I felt like I needed permission before I could participate.

"Yes, I am, you must be Sidney," Rawiri held out his hand. "Welcome to the Christchurch Heroes. They're just warming up now."

The first training session did not last long as it began to rain shortly after I arrived.

My first time on the field playing rugby was the pre-season game against the Vipers from the Burnside Rugby Football Club. Once again, I could feel my heart pounding in my chest. I was on the wing, but I was too slow, unfit, and unskilled. I only managed to initiate one tackle.

"You did well, young man. You need to learn to trust yourself. You need to learn to harness and control your aggression. If you don't commit yourself fully, the only person who'll get hurt is yourself," Mark the medic told me after the game.

We lost by a massive margin. I felt defeated. This sense of defeat continued over the course of the next two years, but we persisted. We experienced the best, and the worst.

Now that I was aware of how my identity occupies intersecting marginalisation in society as a Queer and Asian person, this taught me to navigate the world with fear – I had to make the conscious effort to take up spaces where people like me were regularly excluded.

I still clearly remember the remarks coming from the opposition sideline when we were playing against the Wankers from Shirley Rugby Football Club:

"Go home faggots!"

"Get off the field gaybos!"

"Poofters!"

I knew those people shouting insults at us from the sidelines were not just directing them at my team and me, they were directed at our Queer communities. They did not think we had the right to belong. This only made me want to grow stronger and more resilient.

I still fondly remember the moment we won our first game against the Bullocks at Linwood Rugby Club. It was a tough grind over the eighty minutes. When the referee blew the final whistle, the whole team ran on to the pitch. We had won 17–31.

I learnt that representation could be as simple as being visible.

"You're the first homo I've ever met," a player from the team told me after a game of rugby one Saturday night. He was bent over a fence after throwing up into a bush. "I've never met a gay before, until I met you. You're just a normal guy."

I also learnt that allyship came when I least expected it.

"Do you have any rainbow tape?" another player asked me in a message. "It's International Pride month and I want to acknowledge it at tonight's night game against the Sumner Sharks."

A night game under the floodlights was a special occasion for a social team like ours. We did not normally get the same recognition as the premier teams in the club. I was surprised that a player from my team would want to show his support for our Queer communities.

"Here you go!" the player told me as he handed me a pair of Rainbow laces, as we were getting ready for the game in the changing rooms. "This is the best I could do."

When I was playing touch rugby or rugby union, I felt like I was part of something greater than myself. Who would have known that a simple rugby ball would propel me on my coming out journey?

Reluctant leadership
Ōtautahi, Summer 2019

"Don't forget, the Christchurch Heroes is having its annual general meeting this weekend." Oliver mentioned after a game of touch rugby. We had lost miserably that afternoon. "We can't keep doing this without volunteers."

"I want to help," I later told him at Baillie's, our local bar. Up until this point, I had been a passive beneficiary of other Queer people's goodwill and kindness. I thought of Peters' advice – I must harness my privilege. This is my opportunity to give back to the community.

"Of course," Oliver told me. "We're always looking for volunteers."

After a few short weeks as an elected board member for the Christchurch Heroes, I received a surprise message from Rawiri.

"I'm at a Qtopia strategy meeting at the moment. We were wondering if you'd like to join the board as a treasurer," the message read.

"What have I got to lose?" I thought to myself. If it were not for Qtopia, I would not have had the confidence to explore my Queer identity.

"Of course," I replied to Rawiri. "I'm happy to help where I can."

This was at the start of 2020, just before the first Covid-19 national lockdown. It was not until six months later that I had my first taste of what it meant to be involved in governance. I was there for the annual general meeting, and it was the first time I met the other board members in person.

I sat there in the co-working space feeling somewhat out of place. The only other Asian was the outgoing treasurer. We had met a few times previously to organise the handover. It's not unusual for me to be the only visual minority in a Queer space.

My experience as the social club president at work did not prepare me for this role and the amount of pressure it would involve. One of my first tasks was to organise the financial audit. Due to internal changes and the lack of staffing capacity, this was never completed.

Through this process, I learnt a lot about the financial struggles of a small under-resourced Queer social services provider. I learnt that funding from government agencies is almost exclusively project based and never for more than a year. Although Qtopia has existed for over twenty years, we have never had a sense of financial stability or sustainability. How can our communities, let alone an organisation providing much needed peer-support services, survive in such a precarious financial landscape?

A lot of this has to do with our location in Te Waipounamu – naturally, our Queer communities in Ōtautahi do not have the same benefit as other Queer organisations based in densely populated urban areas like Tāmaki Makaurau or in close proximity to central government like Te Whanganui-a-Tara. In many ways, our Queer population is largely forgotten.

"I would like you two to be our next co-chairs," the managing director asked another board member and me one afternoon. "Christchurch is too white. I want us to change that perspective. We need greater representation for our Queer *rangatahi* (youth) that Queer Brown people exist."

I have not named the other co-chair to protect their privacy, but neither the other co-chair nor I knew what we were signing up to taking up the mantle as co-chairs of Qtopia. As we went through the proceedings of the annual general meeting, with Rawiri chairing the public meeting, both of us were voted in unanimously.

"Now we're coming to the end of the general meeting, does anyone have any general business they would like to share?" Rawiri broadcasted through the computer monitor.

"I do," a group facilitator announced from the group of attendees. "I would like to read a letter of concern from our facilitators."

"Please go ahead," Rawiri signalled from the screen.

"What a way to start our first day on the job, eh?" the other co-chair joked quietly.

I will not go through the details of the letter, but this letter highlighted a number of structural and systemic issues within the youth and social work sector. This turned into an investigation that spanned several months, and it put me and the other co-chair in an uncomfortable position having to address twenty years' worth of organisational debt.

I later found out through the Queer communities that the volunteer facilitators who were present wanted to roll the governance board. I did not even realise that I was at my first coup. We later made robust changes to the constitution at the special general meeting to ensure that nothing of this nature would ever happen again.

I still struggle with my role within Queer spaces. Once at an event with Queer youth and social workers, I doubted my abilities and what I actually contributed within this space.

"I need to tell you something," I confessed to the other co-chair.

The other co-chair sensed something was wrong with me and took me with them to a quiet spot with a couch.

"I don't know if I belong. I don't feel Queer enough. Everyone here is dressed in Rainbows and shit. Maybe I'm the imposter."

"Sidney," the other co-chair told me. "The fact you feel like an imposter is the very reason you belong. As Queer people, as Brown Queer people, we need to show the world we exist."

The other co-chair gave me a hug, firm enough to squeeze out my insecurities.

Many Queer Asian New Zealanders who have contributed and continue to contribute to our communities fly under the radar. Many continue to live a double life as they outwardly express their Queerness in some spaces but are still deeply in the closet at home. These are still unresolved challenges for our Asian communities in Aotearoa.

Content warning

This chapter contains references to homophobia; mental illness and ableism; racism and racial slurs; self-harm and suicidal thoughts, intentions, and actions; substance use and abuse.

The chapter starts overleaf.

11

to love one's imperfections

Ōtautahi, Summer 2019

The first time I met Jake was on the rugby field. Our relationship developed slowly over the course of the touch rugby season. We spoke briefly on the field and at the pub, but what made me attracted to him was his cheeky sense of humour and his tiny rugby shorts.

The first time we spent time alone together, we went for a walk along the rugged coastline of Awaroa (Godley Head). He picked me up from my inner-city apartment. As we made our way along the track we found a dead bird in the bush, a dead seal lying on a rocky beach, and a dead sheep floating off the coast.

"Welcome to the walk of death," Jake joked as we left the track. "Let's get some gelato."

Our relationship did not come to fruition until "Crate Day", which is an unofficial holiday to celebrate the first weekend of summer. It was an excuse to binge drink and your sole purpose for the day was to drink a crate of beer over the course of the day.

Adam, who I met through the Christchurch Heroes, invited me to his house to get drunk.

In all honesty, I do not remember many details from that day. I do remember dancing on the wooden patio with a pair of beige stilettoes on and playing corn hole on the lawn. There was a lot of Mariah, Lady Gaga, and Cher.

At one point in the evening, my emotions caught up with me. Marilyn, who I had also met through the Christchurch Heroes, hugged me and comforted under the clothesline as I told her about my past abusive relationships.

Jake was quietly sitting in the child-size paddling pool. He waded his arms and fingers through the cool water. Back and forth. Back and forth. I slipped into the pool and sat next to him.

"What are you looking at?" I asked Jake.

"Nothing much," he said as he smiled at me. I could see the reflection of the moon on the surface of the water.

Our gazes locked under the moonlight. Once again, time stopped in its tracks.

The next morning, I woke up beside him. We were in Adam's spare bedroom, and all we could hear was the sound of birds chirping and foraging in the garden. It was going to be a warm day.

"How are you feeling this morning?" I asked Jake. He rolled over and kissed me.

"I'm good, I just need to move around and get the booze out of my system." Jake stretched and he got out of bed. He made his way through the ranch slider.

My head was throbbing, but I followed Jake outside anyway. He was lying on the grass, and I lay down next to him. We listened to the birds as we bathed in the morning sun. Understandably, we had a lazy morning and we finally left Adam's house around midday.

"Are you up to much tomorrow night?" he asked me as he dropped me off at my apartment. "How about a first date?"

Living in a bubble
Ōtautahi, Summer 2020

Jake and I had our first date at Little High Eatery. We ordered *anticuchos* and *Pollo a la Brasa* from El Fogón to share and a *caipirinha* each from Caribe Latin Kitchen.

After dinner, Jake and I sat on the banks of Ōtākaro (Avon River) while we ate ice cream. It was the perfect date. I brought Jake back to my inner-city apartment and we spent the night together. I could only describe these first few days as magical.

Within weeks, we were in a relationship, but we both wanted to take things slowly. Jake ended his long-term relationship, so we were going to spend the first year navigating what it meant for us as a couple. However, fate had other plans in store for us.

It was the early days of the Covid-19 outbreak. The initial cases of the pandemic had been recorded in Wuhan (武漢). An unfortunate consequence of this was a gradual increase of anti-Asian discrimination. I still remember one incident during rugby training.

"We need to start thinking about nicknames," the team manager and fullback shouted at our team as we stood around in a circle after rugby training.

"How about we call Sid, 'Corona'?" Oliver chuckled. "You heard me, right, 'Corona'!" "That's enough," Jake told Oliver sternly. He saw from my expression that I was uncomfortable.

I drank my Lion Brown. I felt grateful that Jake was there to stand up for me. I pretended I heard nothing and let the comment slide. I hoped no one else had heard Oliver's comment.

Besides the increase of anti-Asian discourse, we did not understand the severity of the situation until March 2020, when we received an emergency alert on our phone.

"From 11:59pm tonight, the whole of New Zealand moves to Covid-19 Alert Level 4. Where you stay tonight is where YOU MUST stay from now on. It is likely level 4 measures will stay in place for a number of weeks. Kia kaha."

"Are you watching the announcement?" Jake messaged me while I was at work. Everyone was glued to their devices watching the Prime Minister deliver her update on the outbreak.

"Yeah, I'm okay. I'm just about to go into a meeting. Are you okay?"

At the meeting, our managers instructed us all to go home immediately and to take whatever office equipment we needed. I cautiously hugged my colleagues as I said goodbye - who knew when we would see each other again.

"Do you want to move in with me?" Jake proposed to me as I left the office. Guaranteed cuddles every night! You are my designated SID – self-isolation daddy."

I was at the liquor store when I received Jake's message. I was just about to buy Jake some gin for his birthday which was not for another month. If I was already thinking that far ahead, I suppose there was no harm in moving in with Jake.

"Well, who knew all it'd take was a global pandemic for me to move in with you!" I agreed without thinking twice.

Within hours, I moved in with Jake. Jake was living with three gay men – unbeknownst to me, everyone in the flat was Queer! Since everyone had to stay at home, the closet became my safe haven. I was safe from my ex-partner and my family.

My greatest challenge during lockdown was still working from home while Jake and the rest of his flat were waiting for life to return to some form of normality. As public servants, we were expected to support the Covid-19 response.

I was asked to provide census data at low-level geographies to hapu and iwi. This was computationally expensive and my Surface Pro would struggle with my requests. While the data loaded at a glacial pace, I spent the time to see what Jake was doing downstairs.

I set up my computer in Jake's room and for the first days, I would roll out of bed and begin extracting data. I felt like I was stuck in a time loop. Jake helped me move my workstation to the spare room, which gave me some reprieve from the cabin fever.

"Aren't you meant to be working? For someone meant to be at work, you sure are taking a lot of breaks," Jake joked after my umpteenth visit. He was playing *Animal Crossing*, which was surely more exciting than watching my computer struggle with the program.

I returned to my desk upstairs. I sat there and watched my data load on the screen. I was overcome with emotion as I internalised Jake's comment. I was upset. In the past, I would have bottled my emotions, but we were now living together and there was nowhere for me to hide.

"I need to tell you something. I felt hurt by what you just said," I admitted to Jake, a lump forming in my throat. "I'm stressed and I'm tired. The last thing I want to do is work while the world is falling apart around us."

Jake put down the controller and looked at me. I started to cry.

"I'm sorry, cutie," Jake said apologetically. "I was just joking. I didn't want to upset you."

Eventually, we developed a healthy routine. We explored suburban Ōtautahi on our daily walks. We cooked dinner as a couple, and we spent the evenings together watching classic movies. Our relationship developed organically over the course of the lockdown. We learnt about each other's likes and dislikes. We learnt about ways to communicate difficult topics. We learnt to trust each other. We learnt about what it means to be in a relationship.

As the alert levels decreased, the number of Covid-19 restrictions loosened over time. We returned to our workplaces and slowly expanded our social circles. We were all scared of what it meant to live in the "new normal", but I had Jake to navigate this "new normal" with me.

The highlight of this period was our first road trip beyond Ōtautahi. We ventured across the island to Te Tai Poutini (West Coast) and meandered through the mountain passes. Te Ika-a-

Maui was still in lockdown at the time, so it was just the road and us.

We held hands walking down the foreshore of Hokitika. We explored a replica Chinese garden we found on the lake-bed of a forgotten mining town. We played Ur on the beach while being stung by annoying sand flies at Awarua (Haast). We watched gangs of mischievous kea (mountain parrot) attack unsuspecting vehicles.

"I love you," Jake reminded me as we drank our morning coffee under the splendour of Piopiotahi (Milford Sound).

"I love you, too."

One step at a time
Te Awakairangi, Autumn 2021

As we returned to life under the new normal, I could no longer hide my relationship from my family. I owed it to myself and to Jake to tell my parents about our relationship.

On my first trip back to Te Whanganui-a-Tara since the start of the Covid-19 lockdown, I stayed with my parents in Te Awakairangi. I had to tell them about my relationship with Jake. It was now or never. No more secrets.

「我想話畀你聽我拍緊拖.」 (I'm dating someone.) I told Mum at the dining table.

「哦.」 (Oh.) Mum was surprised. She was not expecting this from me.

「我同個男仔一齊.」 (It's with a boy.)

「係咩.」(Really?)

「係.」(Yes.)

「咁呀。你唔驚因果報應咩.」(Is that so? You're not worried about bad karma.) This was Mum's final attempt to dissuade me.

Of course, I knew this was not entirely true. I knew for a fact diverse expressions of gender and sexuality were not wrong or immoral within Taoism (Siker, 2006). Neither was it sinful in terms of Confucianism or Buddhism. Mum was just trying to find a reason to justify her disapproval.

I knew there was an expectation for children and their descendants to support them in old age. I knew at the back of her mind, Mum wondered who would burn incense for her and Dad once they passed away.

After I told my parents about Jake, I noticed they became less affectionate. Neither were shy of showing public displays of affection, but the hugs and kisses were now replaced with curious questions. Once again, I was happy with tolerance, if acceptance was not attainable.

「你有冇嘢想同我講？」(Do you have anything you want to tell me?) Mum asked me.

I was once again in Te Whanganui-a-Tara for work. We were having breakfast at home. It was the first time Mum and I had had some alone time together since I had told her about Jake. Thankfully, there were no prying eyes or ears.

「你想問咩呀.」(What would you like to ask?) I replied.

「冇嘢好問.」(I've got nothing to ask.) Mum interjected quickly.

We went back to our breakfasts and ate in silence. I had nothing to hide. If Mum had any questions about me or my relationship, she was more than welcome to ask them.

「佢大定你大呀.」 (Who's older?) Mum asked a question.

「佢大過我.」 (He's older.) I answered the question.

「邊個賺多錢呀.」 (Who earns more?) Mum asked another question.

「我人工高過佢.」 (I've got a higher salary.) I once again answered the question.

It did not take long before Jake and I tested positive for Covid-19. We were on the first day of our next road trip on the Te Tau Ihu (Northern South Island) when Jake developed symptoms. We drove back to Ōtautahi to isolate. After a night of restless sleep, I tested positive the next morning.

「喂，我中左招呀.」 (Hello? I've caught it.) I told Mum over the phone.

「咩咁唔少心呀,」 (You should've been more careful.) Mum responded.

I felt terrible, and I expected Mum to continue scolding me for my carelessness.

「至少你有人照顧你呀.」 (At least you've got someone to look after you.). Mum told me.

She told me to take care and hung up.

Success. At least Mum acknowledged my partner. Even though I was sick with Covid-19 symptoms, this felt like a light at the end of the tunnel. I knew it would take time for her to unlearn and relearn her expectations of me, but at least she was beginning this journey.

After the second national lockdown, I was in Te Whanganui-a-Tara for less than a day. I had a few hours before my flight back to Ōtautahi, so I met with Mum and my brother for dinner on Courtney Place.

「好耐冇同你講心事喝.」(We haven't had a heart-to-heart in a long time.) Mum exclaimed loudly at the Chinese restaurant.

「你又咩想問呀.」(What would you like to ask?) I asked her inquisitively.

I knew Mum wanted to ask me about my relationship, but she did not have the vocabulary. I was only going to volunteer the information according to her comfort levels. There was no point forcing her to accept my Queer identity unless she was open to listening.

「冇呀，食完飯先再講.」(Nothing. Let's eat first.) Mum responded.

Maybe next time. We continued with our meal eating what felt like the worst Chinese food in Te Whanganui-a-Tara. She did not ask me any more questions for the rest of the night.

As our relationship progressed, Jake introduced me to his friends, a trans husband and wife duo. She is a community advocate, published celebrity chef, and drag artist. Her husband is the salt of the earth and would rather spend time working the soil than socialising – much like Jake.

"I don't know what it's like to have culture issues to deal with, my parents adapted instantly to me, and then instantly to my wife," Jake's friend messaged me after spending a day gardening with Jake.

"I hope your parents can come to the point of acceptance and see how happy you are. We love how happy you and Jake are."

I was so heartened to see these words of support. It was honestly a privilege to meet older Queer people at this stage of my coming out journey. They were trailblazers who fought fiercely for our Queer communities. It helped me put into perspective my personal struggles. It also taught me why we need to continue advocating for our communities so we can live authentically.

Circuit breaker
Ōtautahi, Summer 2022

We were speeding down Bealey Avenue on New Year's Day. It was 5 o'clock in the morning and the sun was on the cusp of rising over the horizon. Sam was dropping me home from the New Year's Eve party at a mutual friend's home.

"Jake always laugh at my quirks, like the funny names I give objects or the specific ways I needed things done. We normally have a routine before bed where I need him to scratch my back before I roll him over to spoon him," I told Sam as we sped down Bealey Avenue. "He also gets mad that I've got ten conversations going through my head at all times. I've always been like that."

I could not help but laugh.

"Have you considered that you might be neurodivergent?" Sam asked me from the driver's seat. "You should check it out."

"Don't be silly!" I replied drunkenly. I was already Queer and Asian – how many more intersecting marginalisation in society could I possibly occupy?

As the weeks progressed, I started to take Sam's comments more seriously. I started reading up about neurodiversity and the symptoms associated with a neurodivergent brain.

「雖然你讀言語學，點解你溝通能力咁渣架.」 (Even though you study linguistics, why are your communication skills so bad?) Mum asked me time and time again.

One day, I stormed downstairs to see Jake after another heated phone call with Mum.

"I don't know what's wrong with me?" I exclaimed to Jake. "I feel like I try my best to talk to my parents, but I still feel like I'm failing as their son. Sam mentioned it might be because I'm neurodivergent – I could be autistic or have ADHD. I think that's why I've struggled with maintaining relationships my whole life."

"Don't be silly, cutie," Jake told me reassuringly. "Every brain is wired a little bit differently. Don't worry about it. You're fine just the way you are."

I knew Jake was trying to comfort me, but I wanted to retreat into my thoughts. I was once again transported back to the days when I first came out to myself. I was reminded of the countless evenings I would get drunk to the point I would throw up. I would wake up in the morning dry-mouthed and hungover. I was addicted to that sensation because it gave me a reason not to commit to anything or anyone. Once again, I felt like I was back "in a closet".

"I would like to talk to you about ADHD," I mentioned to my family doctor near the end of our appointment. I went to see him after experiencing chronic pain in my abdomen. Neither the X-ray nor ultrasound found anything unexpected with my health.

"Well, I doubt they would've missed this during the early childhood screening," he told me matter-of-factly. "It's quite trendy at the moment. I doubt they'd accept you through public referrals unless it's a life-or-death situation."

"Have you considered going private?" my doctor asked me before escorting me out of the room. "It'll cost you a bit, but you might find the answers you're looking for."

I felt emotionally shattered. It seemed like there was nothing I could do. When I returned to the office, I went online and sent through an assessment request.

"It'll be $150 for the initial screening. If we suspect you have ADHD, then the assessment with a psychologist will be $400," the clinical administrator informed me. "Following that, if you require treatment, it'll be $645 for a medication consultation with a psychiatrist and ongoing costs with a coach and your family."

If that was the price I had to pay for closure, then I had no other choice. I was very privileged at the time because I had a full-time job. My only stumbling block was the screening assessment.

It required at least one person who could provide information on my difficulties and behaviours during childhood and current symptoms.

I considered asking my brother or Jake, but I felt such a deep sense of shame of already being Queer to even entertain the idea

I was neurodivergent. I sat on the initial screening assessment phase for six months before I finally decided to withdraw my assessment.

"Do you have a friend, colleague, or partner that could complete the assessment?" the administrator from the clinic asked me. We had been corresponding for six months at that point. I felt like such a failure.

I sent the assessment to my friend who had recently been through the process. Within days I received another email inviting me to a psychology assessment.

"I've always felt different growing up," I told the psychologist. "I always felt misunderstood. When I was in kindergarten, I remember biting another student because they were mean to me."

"I remember being put in speech therapy because my teachers suspected I had developmental difficulties, but they blamed it on my migrant background and my heritage language."

"I always struggled to maintain friendships. In intermediate school I stopped talking to people because I figured no one understood me anyway."

"My parents complain I don't communicate properly. They always joke about how I was told off by the instructor during swimming lessons because I was too distracted."

"My partner told me I don't pay attention to him, and I'm worried this will put a strain on our relationship. He says I always start conversations in the middle without warning."

"I've recently started my PhD, and some days I really struggle. I would stare at my computer or get distracted by housework or other projects. I'm constantly stressed, and I've only managed to do three hours work in the last week."

"I'm more stressed now than when I was still juggling my full-time job, Certificate in te reo Māori, the work I do in the community, finishing my second master's, and starting my PhD."

"Wow." The psychologist's expression said it all. "Let's get you the help you need."

It was a week before Christmas; I was having lunch with my colleagues from the research office when I received the email from the clinic. I opened the attachment to the email as my colleagues talked about their holiday plans. I skimmed through the report and read the diagnosis.

"In conclusion, Mr Wong's presentation, self-report, available collateral information and the endorsement of items on the inventories and questionnaires used in this assessment are consistent with a diagnosis of: F90.2 Attention Deficit Hyperactivity Disorder, Combined Presentation."

Relief. Finally, an answer to a problem I did not know I had. I felt vindicated, but then I also felt a sense of grief. I grieved for the missed opportunities, the impulsive decisions, and the blame I had experienced up until that point in my life. All might've been avoided had I received this diagnosis. I was briefly sent back to that very moment when I had kissed Iain in the garden all those years ago. Clarity. Enlightenment. Fear.

Jake was busy planning Christmas lunch. He mentioned the dishes he wanted to cook and how he wanted to decorate the flat for Christmas. My mind was occupied with the diagnosis.

"Are you listening to me, cutie?" Jake asked me. "You don't seem to be interested in what I'm saying. Is everything okay?"

Jake seemed distressed. He sometimes worried that my erratic behaviour was a response to what he had done. I did not want him to feel that he was to blame. If I were to make this relationship work, I could no longer hide secrets from Jake.

"I need to tell you something important," I confessed to Jake. "I've been seeking help, but I've been too scared to tell you. I've got ADHD."

I handed Jake my phone with the assessment report. I watched him read the report on my phone. When he finished, he handed my phone back to me.

"I'm sorry. Are you mad at me?" I told Jake apologetically.

"Why would I be mad at you?" Jake told me. "I love you. And I'm sorry that you felt like you couldn't come to me to talk about this."

With Jake's blessing, I continued with my treatment plan and met with a psychiatrist. I was prescribed methylphenidate to balance the chemicals in my brain.

"We're going to see each other a lot now you've received your diagnosis, " my family doctor told me. "It's not going to be a straightforward process. There's a lot of restrictions around controlled drugs to make sure you're not abusing them."

I nodded. This was another difficult path I was willing to take.

"Well, why don't we get started with a surprise drug test."

Content warning

This chapter contains references to abuse; death, dying, and mass murder; hateful behaviour directed at religious groups; homophobia; nudity; racism and racial slurs; substance use and abuse; transphobia; and violence.

The chapter starts overleaf.

12
to stand without faltering

Mumbai, Winter 2022

"I'm proud of you. You've come a long way.," Ashish told me. It was in the early hours of the morning, and we were now alone in our twin-single hotel room.

"I think we both have," I told him as I drank another sip of the cherry-flavoured RTD (alcopop). This was not my beverage of choice, but it was what was left in the mini-bar.

We were reminiscing about the adventures we had had together over the years. We talked about how we met, the people we've met, the arguments we've had. At one point we shed drunken tears as we thought about our futures and what was in store for us.

Earlier that night, Ashish, Neil, and I were sampling the bars in Bandra West. We went to the Bar Stock Exchange where the price of beer would rise and fall based on popularity. We tried to enter the Escobar, but they required a cover charge of ₹3,000 each. This was the price of being in a group of "straight" and "single" men.

We ended up at Toto's Bar, an auto-garage themed dive bar playing classic rock music. The bar was packed, and we had nowhere to sit. We were offered a place to stand near the entrance to the kitchen.

"We knew you were gay," Neil confessed to me. "We wanted to give you the time you needed to process whatever you were going through."

"We were so close, man," Neil told me. We were all getting noticeably drunk. "You were the only one that took us to parties in Christchurch. But it's okay, I knew we would spend time together again at some point. I wouldn't have guessed Bandra West, but here we are."

Kanta extended an invite to a drag party at Kitty Su. Neil decided to stay at the dive bar, so Ashish and I took an auto rickshaw to Andheri.

When we arrived at the bar, the party was already in full swing. There were 50 to 100 people in the club. We were in the basement bar of a hotel. Besides the sign with a Pride flag, no one would've known there was a drag show here.

"Please forgive me, it's a really small party," Kanta told us as he came to greet us at the door.

The venue gave me a sense of déjà vu. We could have been in Ōtautahi, and I would have believed it. Everyone there, young and old, was dancing. I recognised the coat check at the entrance for people to store their day clothes while they changed into something that felt more authentic.

"I would never expect to see something like this," Ashish told me as he walked towards me in a daze. He had just taken a shot from the crotch of a go-go boy. "In India of all places!"

The night was cut short just after midnight. It was Republic Day which is a designated dry day in the state of Maharashtra.

"I can get you some booze from the black market if you want, sweetie," Amitabh offered as he approached me for a kiss. I gently pushed him away.

"He thinks you're from the North East," Kanta told me discreetly. "I think you're his type." "Mate, you got to take one for the team," Ashish joked. He always told me I could pass as aNorth East Indian. I found it ironic that I was exotified whether I was home or abroad.

The night was getting late. Kanta hailed his driver, and we headed back to Bandra West. Amitabh made it into the car, but Ashish kindly created a human barrier between us before dropping him off on the side of the road. It was nearly three o'clock in the morning before we finally arrived back at the hotel.

"I never wanted this," I confessed to Ashish. "I just wanted to live a normal life."

"I don't think 'normal' was ever a choice when you came out to me all those years ago," Ashish told me. He drank a blue liquor from a glass. We were drinking whatever we could find in the fridge. It was nearly five o'clock. We had a wedding to attend in ten hours.

Our darkest day
Tāmaki Makaurau, Autumn 2021

I was invited to represent Qtopia at a meeting in Tāmaki Makaurau for the Royal Commission of Inquiry's Report into the terrorist attack on the Al Noor Mosque and Linwood Islamic Centre in Ōtautahi. This meeting was organised by the Department of the Prime Minister and Cabinet (DPMC) to address the impacts of the terrorist attack on Queer communities.

We listened to the experiences of Queer Muslims who were invited by Rainbow Path NZ. They are an organisation dedicated to advocating, supporting, and promoting the rights of Queer refugees and asylum seekers in Aotearoa.

When it was my turn to talk, I realised that I was the only person from Ōtautahi in the room. I stood up to speak, and I started to cry as I retold my version of events.

It was an unassuming Tuesday afternoon. I was at the office in the central city, and I could not wait to go home. It was around 1:45pm when I received the first notification on my phone.

"Developing situation in Christchurch," read the headline. "Police are responding to reports of shots fired in central Christchurch at around 1:40pm."

Within minutes, rumours began to circulate around the office. Someone mentioned that there was a heist in the central city. Another person mentioned that there was a co-ordinated terrorist attack making its way through the city.

"My brother told me they can hear gunshots at CPIT," Bob told me as he watched his phone. Everything was happening in real time. "They're currently locked in the building. He told me they've been asked to hide under their desks. What's going on? Is he going to be okay?"

Owen tried to leave the building with his swipe card. The door would not budge. "I think we're locked in as well." Owen told us.

This was confirmed shortly after when we received an email from building services: "Our building is now in lockdown. Our advice is for everyone to stay in the building. Please refrain from leaving the building and stay away from the windows at this time."

I found an empty meeting room to call Rakim.

"I don't know what's happening, but I think I'm safe where I am," I whispered to Rakim.

"They say people are killing Muslims in Christchurch," he told me. "Will I be safe in Ōamaru?" The next update I saw was on my Facebook feed.

"A man came into the mosque near Christchurch's Hagley Park with an automatic rifle and shot people, a witness says. Schools are in lockdown and people are told to stay inside in the area."

I went online and began listening to updates on Radio New Zealand from my computer. We were told that the armed offender's squad was deployed, and they were stationed around Christchurch Hospital and all government buildings. In that moment, Bob and I burst into tears. Neither of us had ever been caught amidst an active shooter situation. We did not know what to do or how to react.

"There's a wedding party locked in with us in the building," Owen informed me. We had a chapel in the foyer of the building for officiating marriages.

"What bar stocks do we have?" I asked Owen as I came to grips with our current situation. I was the president of the social club in the building, and we had the most resources available. We could be locked in the building indefinitely. "Whatever food, drinks, or alcohol we have, let's distribute it among the floors of the building we have access to – especially the wedding party. I think we all deserve a drink to process what's going on."

We were finally let out of the building at around six o'clock in the evening. We were told to evacuate the city centre immediately. There was no public transport as it was being diverted from the city centre. Bob took me back to his home. His mum brought us some sausage rolls as we watched Adventure Time in the guest room. Neither of us had any appetite.

All it took was 12 minutes for a terrorist to take the lives of 51 innocent people. This event exposed the underbelly of white supremacy in Ōtautahi and Aotearoa.

"Have you seen the video?" Becky, my flatmate, asked me as I walked through the door when I finally got home at around 9 o'clock.

"Why would anyone want to watch that?" I replied in disgust. The first question she asked me was whether I had watched the livestream of the shooting. She sent a copy of the manifesto to our flat chat. I immediately deleted the message from my phone. Hate speech does not deserve a platform. I went to my room, and I crashed on my bed. I called Rakim to tell him that I was safe.

"Will this happen in Ōamaru? Will this happen to me?" Rakim asked me.

"I don't know." I did not know what else to tell him. "I think you should avoid coming to Christchurch for the next few weeks."

"I don't want to come to Christchurch anymore. I don't want to be around white people," Rakim told me. I understood his position.

As I recalled my experiences, the public servants in the room looked shocked and visibly uneasy. It dawned on me that the Queer experience in Tāmaki Makaurau and Te Whanganui-a-

Tara was vastly different from those in Ōtautahi. We were invisible.

"I'm sorry," the commissioner responded. "We haven't considered the relevance this event has had on Ethnic Rainbow communities."

Decentring whiteness
Ōtautahi, Spring 2022

As I continued to co-chair Qtopia, I struggled to see myself as a community advocate or activist. I did not feel like I had the right academic foundation, the policy expertise, or the established relationships many Queer advocates and activists had curated over time. There were also times when I felt like an imposter, like I did not belong.

I still remember one strategy day when we were discussing education and development opportunities to upskill our board members. A former board member who was then affiliated to a prominent Queer organisation mentioned that there was an upcoming international conference that would be a great place to network with other Queer advocates and activists.

"We have scholarships on offer to attend this conference," he offered to the group. "I'm happy to provide people with a reference."

I was intrigued by the opportunity to upskill, so I approached him after the strategy day before I was quickly shut down.

"I don't think your voice is necessarily what we need right now," he told me blankly.

"If my voice is not necessarily what is needed, then why am I wasting my time here?" I thought to myself bitterly.

When I first entered the non-profit governance space, I held the naive view that I would be directly supporting our communities. Instead, I spend a majority of my time pandering to funders like central and local government agencies so our staff and volunteers could provide their support services without distraction. One thing that is not mentioned enough in non-profit governance is the amount of work needed to maintain our legal status as a charity.

We would spend countless hours working through funding applications, charitable returns, and financial audits when we could be using our time and energy to develop services. I understand that the purpose of these checks and balances is to ensure transparency, but the amount of scrutiny charitable organisations is under seems excessive considering the little funding we receive. I went from being paid as a public servant to process these forms to just being a member of the public doing this voluntarily.

Beyond the copious amounts of bureaucratic hurdles, I struggled with the amount of jargon needed to understand what was going on during a board meeting. I had no idea what people meant when we had to go "in committee" or why we had to "make a motion". We were also expected to act professionally, or be kind, and speak of safe spaces. At times, I truly wondered whether these processes were put in place to exclude people from being able to support their communities without the right resources or the right connections.

As fate would have it, that meeting organised by the DPMC placed me on the radar of other Queer organisations. More importantly, I had the rare opportunity to connect with Queer non-white tauiwi (non-Māori) advocates. For the lack of better terminology, we were beginning to rally under the broad Queer Ethnic or Ethnic Rainbow banner. We recognised that we were a diverse group of Queer people from ethnic, migrant, or former refugee backgrounds.

I was truly fortunate to speak with one Queer Ethnic advocate candidly about my experience of trying to navigate this non-profit service provision space. I still remember when they told me quite clearly, "Professionalism is just shorthand for whiteness." A similar process of racialisation was also occurring in the governance of our Queer communities – if it is even possible to govern a community that is fluid, inclusive, undefined, and ever-evolving. I now know why I had to modify my behaviour to be palatable in these governance spaces. As a racialised Queer person, I was once again expected to assimilate with the dominant norms of Pākehā whiteness.

What I remember most distinctly from the DPMC meeting was the lack of Queer Muslim attendees at the meeting. This was odd considering that we were there specifically to discuss the impacts of the terrorist attack on people who occupied this extremely specific intersection. Instead, Queer advocates dominated it, largely Pākehā, who had the audacity to speak on the behalf of the whole Rainbow community. We were watching the process of racialisation unfold before our eyes.

I now know why the former board member of a prominent Queer organisation told me why my voice was not necessarily needed right now. My voice was not the white voice he wanted to represent us. I am confident that I am not the only racialised Queer person who has been gate-kept/door-kept from sharing our perspectives. Why do we need to benchmark our diverse Queer identities with whiteness? If we do not centre our diverse needs, we will remain invisible.

Some of those Queer advocates co-founded the Ethnic Rainbow Alliance (ERA) so that we as a diverse community can begin to create our own spaces. Once again, I was truly fortunate that the co-founders asked me to chair ERA. There was not much we could do to decentre whiteness in a pre-existing organisation. What we can do is centre our perspectives at all times.

Within weeks of establishing a trust board and being registered as a charitable organisation, ironically, systems and structures grounded in whiteness – we were asked to provide advice to central and local government agencies.

"We want to know how we can support our Ethnic Rainbow communities," a representative from the ministry asked me.

"I'm simply curious. Have you ever been abused in your relationships? I read some literature on high rates of domestic abuse in same-sex relationships?"

I was stunned by her question. I answered her honestly, but I felt shameful and embarrassed as I entertained her with my misery porn. I walked away from that meeting emotionally bruised. I found a quiet booth to cry in.

"I never chose to be an advocate for our Queer communities," I spluttered to Dan on the phone. "How can I call myself an advocate when I'm still broken?"

We are still in the early days of ERA. No one said that it would be easy. I know that it will be tough and bruising work, but I hope we can begin to see our diverse perspectives uplifted to decentre whiteness from our Queer communities in Aotearoa even if it takes one conversation at a time.

Stand in solidarity
Ōtautahi, Summer 2023

Once again, it was Pride week in Ōtautahi. I was on the way to the Qtopia ball when I received a message through my direct message on Twitter. The day before, I was at the opening event where I walked alongside 700 people on Cashel Street in support of our Queer communities.

"Can you please spread this message through your networks?" the message requested. "Police and security are aware that unpleasant people might try to disrupt the Story Time, so we are not expecting to have to get in the way of them physically. We want to avoid confrontation." "We're looking for people to join with us at the Drag Story Time at Tūranga tomorrow to have a positive presence that counters a potentially unpleasant presence of far-right individuals. We want to help ensure it is a safe and friendly experience for parents and children, so the goal is not to have confrontation or appear like a protest, so the intention is to keep our presence low-key if possible." "I think we should go tomorrow," I told Jake as we pulled up to park. "Your friends are performing at the Drag Race Story Time, and I'm worried they might be in danger."

I arrived at the Christchurch Art Gallery, and I watched the hundreds of Queer young people line up to enter the venue. I knew that many of these young people had been anticipating for this one night every year where they could be themselves. The Pride march from the day before had led me into a false sense of security. What was meant to be a night of Queer affirmation turned into dread as I worried what the future had in store for these young people.

The next day, Jake and I arrived at the public library neighbouring Cathedral Square to a crowd of 30 protesters. Most of them were in black and they were ready and poised with their loudspeakers and placards to direct hate at our friends who were inside reading storybooks.

"Drag Pedos Groom Kids."

"Teach Maths not Masturbation."

I could not believe the messages they were directing at the children and their families attending this event which was promoting diversity and inclusion. Thankfully, there was an even larger crowd of counter protesters made up of members from our Queer communities and allies from our local anti-fascist group. Many of the Christchurch Heroes received the message from the night before and were prepared to protect our communities.

Jake and I joined the human barrier between the protesters and the venue. It was a surreal experience. I felt a sense of sadness and anger as we stood there counter protesting the far-right extremists at Queens Telling Stories. I felt a sense of rage that I had not felt before in my life – not even when I had needed to harness my aggression on the rugby field.

Not long into the event, the leaders of the protesters began their sermon of hate. Some of the counter protesters wanted to engage and reason with the far-right extremists in extended debates that went nowhere. Others printed signs saying "Dicks" with an arrow pointing at them to mock them for their misguided crusade.

"Just turn our backs to them," the chairperson of Christchurch Pride instructed the counter protesters. "They're narcissists. If they want a platform, let's not give them one."

I was seething. Jake and I were not interested in engaging. We just wanted to make sure our friends, the children, and their families were safe.

A few teenage protesters broke into the venue and briefly disrupted the event before they were escorted out of the venue. They were presumably children of the far-right protesters. The only grooming that was happening that day was from the fascist transphobes.

Once we heard that our friends, the drag artists, and the children and their families had been safely escorted out of the library, we quickly disbanded. Our purpose was fulfilled, and we did not need to give the fascists a platform. One of the more heartwarming stories came from within the room that we had been trying to safeguard.

"Why are people mean?" one of the children at the event innocently asked our friend in drag who was reading to the children. This question was in response to the disruptive protesters who had invaded the room with their hate and bigotry.

"Well, this is because sometimes when people don't understand something that's different, they get mean," my friend replied to the inquisitive group of children, "but how do we help them? With kindness and love!"

I took this as a sign there is still hope for our future generations to create a more inclusive society, but we cannot achieve this without continued support for our transgender communities.

Peace was short-lived when we received news of a women's rights activist group coming to Aotearoa and spreading their transphobic rhetoric in Tāmaki Makaurau and Te Whanganui-a-Tara. Fortunately, Ōtautahi was spared the transphobes' crusade of hate, but this event empowered the fundamentalist church.

Within days, I received an invitation to a rally outside the Bridge of Remembrance.

"We encourage our community to rally together and if you are an ally this is your time to show your true support and allyship. Being an ally is more than just changing your logo to a rainbow or dancing at our parties. Transphobia is alive and well, this is our opportunity and responsibility to say there is no room for it here in Aotearoa!"

I sent a message to one of the organisers to see if they needed any support.

"We could do with some marshals to control the crowd," the organiser told me. "The event has snowballed into something bigger than we expected."

"At least now we know there's still love in our communities," I told him.

"You're right," he responded before sending through some instructions.

As I was busy wrangling marshals who were willing to help at the rally, the staff and board members of Qtopia were doing what they needed to organise health and safety and mental health first aid for what was going to be a rally of around 500 and a countless number of counter protesters from far-right and religious fundamentalist groups.

We released funds to purchase water, snacks, and other necessary equipment. The staff also organised a sign-making event the day before so that those most vulnerable from our communities and our young people could be involved without putting themselves in unnecessary harm – all this was organised with a few days' notice.

The day before the rally, Jake and I went to the sign-making event at the Christchurch Art Gallery before our first pre-season game of rugby. We wanted to be there to show our support. When we arrived, the craft room was already packed. Jake did not take any time at all. He traced a heart on a placard.

I thought for a while how I wanted to express my support of our trans communities. I also wanted to make sure that someone reading my message knows that Queer Chinese people exist in Ōtautahi. And then the words struck me: 「屹立不倒」(to stand without faltering). My aspiration for our Queer communities is that will stand tall together without wavering. We will not yield to transphobia or bigotry.

Once we left our placards to dry, we said our farewells and left for Rangiora to play the Southbrook Saracens. Even though it was a friendly game, it was still incredibly tough as the team we were playing were a grade above us. I tried to focus on the rugby and tried not to think about the rally ahead of us.

After 80 minutes of intense rugby through rain and mud, I was sitting in the changing shed with the rest of the team. I was nursing my sore calf with a cold stubby of Speights. We had lost 19–15. I was knackered.

"Well done boys, you all did much better than we expected," the head coach congratulated us. "We've got a few honourable mentions, but the coaches have all decided that the player of the day goes to … Sid Dog!"

The changing shed erupted into applause as the team cheered me on. As is customary, I sculled back the beer I had in my hands. I was ecstatic. I have been learning how to play rugby for the last four years and to receive player of the day recognised how far I had come from the young person who was still one foot "out of the closet" to being a rugby player in a team of people who I had avoided my whole life.

As we made our way home, it dawned on me how much danger we would be getting ourselves into tomorrow at the rally. Just hours earlier, I had received news that far-right protesters had arrived at the rally in Tāmaki Makaurau armed with weapons.

"I'm scared, Jake," I confessed to Jake as we drove home. "These people really hate us. They don't want us to exist. They'd rather we were dead."

I felt a mix of emotions. I was both happy for being recognised as the player of the day and sad for the day that was about to come.

"I don't want you to go. I don't want you to get hurt," I told Jake. "If things turn ugly, someone might get hurt or, worse, get killed."

"I don't either," Jake comforted me. "That's why I want to be there by your side."

"I have no complaints if this was going to be the last day of my life," I reflected to myself as I watched the cars speed past us on the motorway.

Jake and I arrived early the next day to find the Bridge of Remembrance already occupied by the fascists. We covered our hi-vis jackets and made our way to the safety briefing for the marshals.

"Whatever you do, do not engage with the transphobes," one of the organisers told us. "We don't want them to have any footage they can use against us."

"We don't want a repeat of what's happened in Auckland. It's going to be a long day. They've seen your face now, so they know who you are. Just be safe. Make sure you're travelling as a group."

When the rally started, we guided young and vulnerable people to the front of the rally where there were speakers, music, and performers. We escorted parties of supporters across the bridge while avoiding the hate and bigotry of the counter protesters.

We stayed at the back and created a human barrier while the bigots hurled abuse at us.

Over 1,000 people turned up to support our trans communities. Our trans solidarity rally went without incident, but our greatest challenge was yet to come. The transphobes were once again ready to preach their hatred as another rally was organised by the counter protesters to start within minutes after the end of our rally.

"Officially, our rally is now over. If you want to stay to marshal, it is purely up to you," an organiser warned us. "What happens from here is out of our control."

We were effectively countering the counter protesters, and the attendees who were already there were not going to leave without a fight. Within minutes of the preaching, the attendees of the trans solidarity rally roared into life. Everyone was doing what they could to drown out the bigotry. Whistles. Trumpets. Drums. Pots and pans. The sound was deafening.

"They've shown respect to your community and listened to what you had to say," a police officer shouted through the noise. "It's your turn to show them some respect."

"They don't respect us," I thought to myself. "They want us all dead."

Once again, Jake and I, alongside the other marshals, stood between the rally attendees and the counter protesters. We tried everything we could to control the crowd. We signalled. We waved. We instructed.

"Turn around!" "Don't engage!" "Turn around." "Don't engage!"

As the gap between the two groups narrowed, Jake reached out his arm to squeeze my hand.

"I love you, cutie."

"I love you."

Epilogue

Hong Kong, Winter 2005

Mum had brought my brother and me to Wong Tai Sin Temple 黃大仙祠. We had been going through a spate of bad fortune, and Mum wanted us to see a spirit medium. She wanted to know if we had inherited bad 因果 (*jan¹gwo²*; karma) from our previous lives that was impacting us.

Wong Tai Sin 黃大仙 was a healer way back in history. He was elevated to the position of a Taoist Deity in recognition of his miracles. He was known as the Great Deity 大仙. We have an altar dedicated to the Great Deity back in Te Awakairangi.

There were hundreds of booths lined up outside the Temple. It was a popular site in Hong Kong as the Great Deity was best known for 「有求必應」 (ask and it is given). Over centuries, Taoist practitioners developed methods to communicate with our Deities such as 求籤 (kau⁴chim¹; divination sticks) or 筊杯 (*gaau³bui¹*; moon blocks).

We found the correct booth and we sat down in front of an unassuming older woman. The older woman was a renowned ornithomancer. One by one, the spirit medium invited Mum, my brother, and I to have our past, present, and future examined. Our fates were mediated through a little yellow bird and sheets of paper that were meant to come from the Great Deity himself.

After two hours of intense examination, we were each given a cassette tape detailing our fortunes. This was our 三世書 (saam¹sai³syu¹; three generation book). We were told to keep these hidden as it could lead to unnecessary complications if they fell into the wrong hands.

"Change is a natural part of life, and it will come when it comes," the spirit medium told us.

She could tell that Mum was anxious after hearing about all the debts we had inherited from our previous lives.

"Think of your life as different bodies of water, we must learn to adapt to our environment."

"There are times when you must be sudden and aggressive like a wave. Through sheer force alone, even a mighty cliff will crumble to sand."

"There are also times when you must be slow and passive like the water in a well. It may take a long time, but eventually, even a stagnant pool will erode stone walls."

"But change does not need to be aggressive or passive like water in a wave or a well. Neither state is sustainable for change."

"The nature of change can be constant like the water in a stream. Over time, life will carve out its own course in the landscape."

"This is the same for people. We cannot be too aggressive or passive," the spirit medium told us. "We must be constant and react to the environment around us. We can only influence change once we learn how to cultivate *Tao* within ourselves."

***

In the short time I have been on this earth, I have come to realise that life was never about the destination, but the journey. Whether individuals within our Queer Asian communities opt to come out, let in, create a narrative of convenience, or another framework we have yet to define, change is an inevitable part of our identity. Asians have been and will always be woven into the fabric of Aotearoa, but our narratives are often made invisible in a society dominated by whiteness. This is why I encourage all Queer Asians to share their experiences. This is the only way we can highlight the richness of our identity. I hope that reading about my experience will empower Queer Asians across Aotearoa to realise their full potential. Our Queer identities are fluid, inclusive, undefined, and ever-evolving. I have not included a conclusion because we are not yet at the end. Mum would often say 「船到橋頭自然直」 (Circumstances change for the better in the face of adversity). I know this to be true. Now I have shared my most intimate thoughts, I am going to take one more step out of the closet as I continue on this journey called life.

Recommended projects

1. Demonstrate an understanding of how different social, cultural, political, and environmental contexts mediate individual and societal perceptions of Queer identities.

   a. What aspects of your culture such as values and traditions are fundamental to you? How do they influence your understanding of Queer identities?

   b. What is your relationship to the Queer community or members of the Queer community? If you do not have a relationship with the Queer community, explain why that might be the case.

   c. How does your environment impact your relationship with the Queer community? Take into consideration any physical or virtual limitations.

   d. Pick a country and research the rights affecting the Queer community. How has this changed over the course of your lifetime? Pick another country and do the same exercise. How do the two countries differ? Explain why there might be similarities or differences between the two countries.

   e. With reference to the text, explain how the author's social, cultural, political, and environmental contexts, mediated their perception of their Queer identity.

2.   Describe how transcultural and translinguistic expressions of Queerness allow for the (re)emergence of Queer identities.

     a.   How has the demographic make-up of your local area changed? Find the most recent official statistics for your local area and comment on how the demographic landscape has changed over the course of your lifetime. If possible, what is the proportion of Queer-identified population in your local area?

     b.   Choose two familiar languages or language varieties and research corresponding translations of terms describing Queer identities. Now find corresponding translations of terms used by the Queer community. Are the translations of these terms equivalent? What challenges did you face finding the most appropriate translation?

     c.   With reference to the text, explain how the author's cultural and linguistic expressions of Queerness differ from your own understanding of Queerness.

3.   Privilege emerging traditional and Indigenous understandings of Queer identities while challenging the notion of universality in Queer identity models developed within Western academic frameworks.

     a.   Research the traditional and Indigenous peoples of your local area.

     b.   Choose a traditional or Indigenous culture and research a particular facet of Queer identity or expression. Consider differences and similarities with your own cultural background.

c. Choose a traditional or Indigenous culture and consider the impacts of colonisation and imperialism on Queer identities and expression.

d. Choose a historical or contemporary Queer identity model (i.e. Cass identity model, Fassinger's model of gay and lesbian identity development) and research the genealogy of this model. Consider how traditional or Indigenous knowledge has been included or excluded from this model.

e. With reference to the text, explain how traditional and indigenous understandings of Queer identities are included or excluded in your community.

4. Think critically about the impacts of (multi-)marginalisation among members of the Queer community who occupy intersecting marginalisation in society.

a. Discuss diversity, equity, and inclusion within the context of your community.

b. Research Queer physical or virtual spaces in your local area. Describe each of these spaces. How many of these spaces cater to marginalised communities?

c. Consider visible and invisible representation of intersectional Queer identities in the media. Choose three source texts from the same medium (e.g. book, movie, television programme, online article, social media) and describe the type of identities represented. Explain why some identities are more visible than others based on the source text.

d. Identify an intersectional community within your local area and propose human infrastructure and/or services that can be developed to support this community.

e.   With reference to the text, explain how intersectional communities experience multi-marginalisation in your community.

5.   Engage individual lived experiences and perspectives as a vehicle for effective allyship within and outside the Queer community.

a.   Discuss your understanding of what it means to be an effective ally.

b.   Choose a charitable service provider within your local area and discuss what you can do to provide support.

c.   With reference to the text, explain how you can use your lived experiences and perspectives as a vehicle for effective allyship within and outside the Queer community.

Recommended further reading

Ip, M,. ed. (2003). *Unfolding History, Evolving Identity: The Chinese in New Zealand.* Auckland: Auckland University Press.

Luther, J. D. and Loh, J. U, eds. (2019). *Queer Asia: Decolonising and Reimagining Sexuality and Gender.* London: Bloomsbury Publishing.

McEvoy, M. (2022). *30 Queer Lives: Conversations with LGBTQIA+ New Zealanders.* Wellington: Massey University Press.

Rangnekar, S. D. (2022). *Queersapien.* New Delhi: Rupa.

Tecun, A., Lopesi, L., and Sankar, A. eds. (2022). *Towards a Grammar of Race in Aotearoa New Zealand.* Wellington: Bridget Williams Books.

References

Adams, T. E. (2011). *Narrating the Closet: An Autoethnography of Same-Sex Attraction*. New York, NY: Routledge.

Al-Ali, N. and Sayegh, G. (2019). Feminist and Queer perspectives in West Asia: complicities and tensions. In Luther, J. D. and Loh, J. U., eds., *Queer Asia: Decolonising and Reimagining Sexuality and Gender*. London: Bloomsbury Publishing. pp. 245–265.

Broughton, C. (2019). Christchurch's only gay nightclub criticised for declaring staff are known as "barmen". *Stuff*. [Online] Available at: www.stuff.co.nz/business/117481171/christchurchs-only-nightclub-criticised-for-declaring-staff-are-known-as-barmen [Accessed 30 March 2023].

Brown, M. P. (2005). *Closet Space: Geographies of Metaphor from the Body to the Globe*. New York, NY: Routledge.

Butler, P. (1977). *Opium and Gold*. Martinborough: Alister Taylor.

Chan, N. S.-H. (2010). Queering body and sexuality: Leslie Cheung's gender representation in Hong Kong popular culture. In Yau, C., ed., *As Normal as Possible: Negotiating Sexuality and Gender in Mainland China and Hong Kong*. Hong Kong: Hong Kong University Press. pp. 133–149.

Chung, S. F. and Wegars, P. (2005). Introduction. In Chung, S. F. and Wegars, P., eds., *Chinese American Death Rituals: Respecting the Ancestors*. Lanham, MD: Rowman Altamira.

Columbia Law School (2017). *Kimberlé Crenshaw on Intersectionality, More than Two Decades Later*. [Online] Available at: www.law.columbia.edu/news/archive/kimberle-crenshaw-intersectionality-more-two-decades-later [Accessed 30 April 2023].

Corrigan, P. and Matthews, A. (2003). Stigma and disclosure: implications for coming out of the closet. *Journal of Mental Health*, 12(3), pp. 235–248. Available at: www.tandfonline.com/doi/abs/10.1080/0963823031000118221 [Accessed 30 March 2023].

Crenshaw, K. (1989). Demarginalizing the intersection of race and sex: a Black feminist critique of antidiscrimination doctrine, feminist theory and antiracist politics. *University of Chicago Legal Forum*, 1989(1), pp. 139–168. Available at: chicagounbound.uchicago.edu/uclf/vol1989/iss1/8 [Accessed 29 April 2023].

Eldred-Grigg, S. (1984). *Pleasures of the Flesh: Sex & Drugs in Colonial New Zealand, 1840–1915*. Wellington: AH & AW Reed.

Ferguson, P. (2003). *The making of the white New Zealand policy: nationalism, citizenship and the exclusion of the Chinese, 1880–1920*. Doctoral. University of Canterbury.

Han, C.-S. (2009). Introduction to the Special Issue on GLBTQ of Color. *Journal of Gay & Lesbian Social Services*, 21(2–3), pp. 109–114. Available at: www.tandfonline.com/doi/full/10.1080/10538720902771826 [Accessed 30 March 2023].

Henderson, A. (2003). Untapped talents: The employment and settlement experience of skilled Chinese in New Zealand. In Ip, M., ed., *Unfolding History, Evolving Identity: The Chinese in New Zealand*. Auckland: Auckland University Press. pp. 141–164.

Ip, M. (1990). *Home Away from Home: Life Stories of Chinese Women in New Zealand*. Auckland: New Women's Press.

Ip, M. and Murphy, N. (2005). *Aliens at My Table: Asians as New Zealanders See Them*. Auckland: Penguin Group.

Jagose, A. (1996). *Queer Theory: An Introduction*. New York, NY: New York University Press.

Karim, M. (2017). *Racism, Policy and Politics*. Bristol: Policy Press.

Kerekere, E. (2017). *Part of The Whānau: The Emergence of Takatāpui Identity – He Whāriki Takātapui*. Doctoral, Victoria University of Wellington.

Kong, T. S. (2012). A fading Tongzhi heterotopia: Hong Kong older gay men's use of spaces. *Sexualities*, 15(8), pp. 896–916. Available at: journals.sagepub.com/doi/10.1177/1363460712459308 [Accessed 29 April 2023].

Lai, C. H. (1974). *New Zealand's immigration policy towards Asians, 1960–1974: a policy of rational exclusion?* Master. University of Canterbury.

Lau, H., Yeung, G., Stotzer, R. L., Lau, C. Q., and Loper, K. (2017). Assessing the Tongzhi label: self-identification and public opinion. *Journal of Homosexuality*, 64(4), pp. 509–522. Available at: pubmed. ncbi.nlm.nih.gov/27191356/ [Accessed 29 April 2023].

Lee, C. and Ostergard, R. L. J. (2017). Measuring discrimination against LGBTQ people: a cross-national analysis. *Human Rights Quarterly*, 39(1), pp. 37–72. Available at: muse.jhu.edu/article/ 647800/pdf [Accessed 30 March 2023].

Murphy, N. (2003). Joe Lum v. Attorney: the politics of exclusion. In Ip, M., ed., *Unfolding History, Evolving Identity: The Chinese in New Zealand*. Auckland: Auckland University Press. pp. 49–51.

Nakhid, C., Yachinta, C., and Fu, M. (2022). Letting in/"coming out" – agency and relationship for young Ethnic Queers in Aotearoa New Zealand on disclosing queerness. *LGBTQ+ Family: An Interdisciplinary Journal*, 18(3), pp. 281–303. Available at: www. tandfonline.com/doi/abs/10.1080/27703371.2022.2091704 [Accessed 30 March 2023].

Ng, D. (1962). *Ninety Years of Chinese Settlement in New Zealand, 1866 to 1956*. University of Canterbury.

Ng, J. (2003). The sojourner experience: the Cantonese goldseekers in New Zealand, 1865–1901. In Ip, M., ed., *Unfolding History, Evolving Identity: The Chinese in New Zealand*. Auckland: Auckland University Press. pp. 5–30.

Omi, M. and Winant, H. (2015). *Racial Formation in the United States*. 3rd ed. York, NY: Routledge.

Pang, P. (2003). Education, Politics and Chinese New Zealander Identities: The Case of the 1995 Epsom Normal Primary School's 'Residency Clause and English Test'. In Ip, M., ed., *Unfolding History, Evolving Identity: The Chinese in New Zealand*. Auckland: Auckland University Press. pp. 236–257.

Parekh, S. (2003). Homosexuality in India: the light at the end of the tunnel. *Journal of Gay & Lesbian Psychotherapy*, 7(1–2), pp. 145–163. Available at: www.tandfonline.com/doi/abs/10.1300/J236v07n01_09 [Accessed 30 March 2023].

Rangnekar, S. D. (2022). *Queersapien*. New Delhi: Rupa.

Sachdeva, S. (2013). Bar's fee for water sparks row. *The Press*. [Online] Available at: www.stuff.co.nz/the-press/news/8205193/Bars-fee-for-water-sparks-row [Accessed 30 March 2023].

Sankar, A., Lopesi, L., and Tecun, A. (2022). Colonisation and race in New Zealand. In Tecun, A., Lopesi, L., and Sankar, A., eds., *Towards a Grammar of Race in Aotearoa New Zealand*. Wellington: Bridget Williams Books. pp. 27–37.

Semerene, G. (2019). Mithliyy, mithlak: language and LGBTQ activism in Lebanon and Palestine. In Luther, J. D. and Loh, J. U., eds., *Queer Asia: Decolonising and Reimagining Sexuality and Gender*. London: Bloomsbury Publishing. pp. 85–108.

Siker, J. S. (2006). *Homosexuality and Religion: An Encyclopedia*. Westport, CT: Greenwood Press.

Skews-Poole, N. (2017). My cousin Allen. *The Spinoff*. [Online] Available at: thespinoff.co.nz/society/15-08-2017/my-cousin-allen [Accessed 30 April 2023].

Stats NZ (2022). *LGBT+ population of Aotearoa: Year ended June 2021*. [Online] Wellington: Stats NZ. Available at: www.stats.govt.nz/information-releases/lgbt-plus-population-of-aotearoa-year-ended-june-2021/ [Accessed 22 April 2023].

Stewart, J. (2018). Academic theory. In Richards, C., Bouman, W. P., and Barker, M.-J., eds., *Genderqueer and Non-Binary Genders*. London: Palgrave Macmillan. pp. 53–73.

Stuff (2018). Controversy ahead of 10 days of fun and festivities for Christchurch Pride Week. *Stuff*. [Online] Available at: www.stuff.co.nz/the-press/news/101919684/controversy-ahead-of-10-days-of-fun-and-festivities-in-christchurch-pride   [Accessed 30 April 2023].

Thomsen, P. S. (2021). Coming-out in the intersections: Examining relationality in how Korean gay men in Seattle navigate church, culture and family through a Pacific lens. *Journal of Homosexuality*, 68(6), pp. 1015–1036. Available at: www.tandfonline.com/doi/full/10.1080/00918369.2019.1695423 [Accessed 30 March 2023].

Upadhyay, N. (2020). Hindu nation and its queers: Caste, Islamophobia, and de/coloniality in India. *Interventions,* 22(4), pp. 464–480.

Yee, B. (2003). Coping with insecurity: Everyday experiences of Chinese New Zealanders. In Ip, M., ed., *Unfolding History, Evolving Identity: The Chinese in New Zealand*. sAuckland: Auckland University Press. pp. 49–51.

Index